extile

TED BY

NINA BARNETT,
IS JEFFERIES
DORAN ROSS

THE JOURNAL OF
CLOTH AND CULTURE

VOLUME 1
ISSUE 2
SUMMER 2003

ORDERING INFORMATION
Three Issues per volume. One volume per annum.
2003: Volume 1

ONLINE
www.bergpublishers.com

BY MAIL
Berg Publishers
C/O Turpin Distribution (Customer Services Dept)
Blackhorse Road
Letchworth
Herts SG6 1HN
UK

BY FAX
+ 44 (0)1462 483011

BY TELEPHONE
+ 44 (0)1462 672555

FOR ENQUIRIES
email: subscriptions@turpinltd.com

ENQUIRIES
Editorial: Kathryn Earle, Managing Editor
email kearle@berg1.demon.co.uk

Production: Sara Everett, Director
email severett@bergpublishers.com

Advertising: Joanne Hutt,
email jhutt@bergpublishers.com

SUBSCRIPTION DETAILS
Free Online Subscription for Print Subscribers.

Full color images available online.

Access your electronic subscription through
www.ingenta.com or www.ingentaselect.com

Institutional base list subscription price:
US$160.00, £100.00

Individuals' subscription price: US$65.00, £40.00

Berg Publishers is the imprint of
Oxford International Publishers Ltd.

AIMS AND SCOPE

Cloth accesses an astonishingly broad range of human experiences. The raw material from which things are made, it has various associations: sensual, somatic, decorative, functional and ritual. Yet although textiles are part of our everyday lives, their very familiarity and accessibility belie a complex set of histories, and invite a range of speculations about their personal, social and cultural meanings. This ability to move within and reference multiple sites gives textiles their potency.

This journal brings together research in textiles in an innovative and distinctive academic forum for all those who share a multifaceted view of textiles within an expanded field. Representing a dynamic and wide-ranging set of critical practices, it provides a platform for points of departure between art and craft; gender and identity; cloth, body and architecture; labor and technology; techno-design and practice—all situated within the broader contexts of material and visual culture.

Textile invites submissions informed by technology and visual media, history and cultural theory; anthropology; philosophy; political economy and psychoanalysis. It draws on a range of artistic practices, studio and digital work, manufacture and object production.

SUBMISSIONS

Should you have a topic you w like us to consider, please ser an abstract of 300–500 words one of the editors. Notes for Contributors can be found at t back of the journal and style guidelines are available by emailing fhowlett@bergpublishers.com from the Berg website (www.bergpublishers.com).

ISSN: 1475-9756
www.bergpublishers.com

Contents

TORS
nina Barnett and **Janis Jefferies**
artment of Visual Arts
dsmiths College
versity of London
v Cross
don
4 6NW

rnett@gold.ac.uk
feries@gold.ac.uk

Doran Ross
UCLA
Fowler Museum of Cultural History
308 Charles Young Drive
Los Angeles CA 90095-1549
USA

doran@isop.ucla.edu

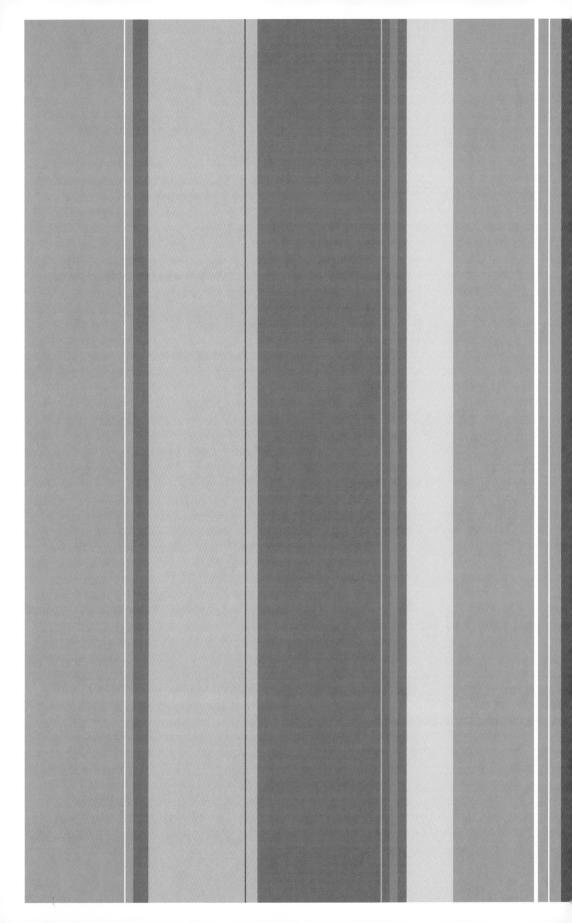

Letter from the Editors

Welcome to the 2nd issue of *Textile: The Journal of Cloth and Culture,* which includes essays and a poem that provoke issues around identity, nation, cinema and computing.

Brenda Danet's essay "Pixel Patchwork: 'Quilting in Time' On Line" references an oft cited motif within discourses around textiles, that of "text" and "textile" as having the same Latin root – textus,or woven. Danet "translates" this motif to digital forms of text-based art that bear a striking similarity to weaving, embroidery and, for her purposes, quilting. Participants in internet relay chat rooms play with patterns and play off ornament in abundant color pixels to produce variations on "quilting in time"—a challenge to traditional notions of art and craft, amateur and professional, signature and authorship. Danet makes a provocative argument for her ethnographic study of an on-line group called "rainbow" to be recognized as an emergent folk art community that mobilizes complex computer skills rather than those of material consequence.

Material skill and the dexterity of stitch are "grounded" in Dorothy Jones' discussion of the production of a 16 meter long embroidery that is housed in Australia's Parliament House in Canberra. Opened in 1988 to celebrate 200 years of the "founding" of Australia, and designed and supervised by one of Australia's most prestigious artists, Kay Lawrence, "Embroidering the Nation" gives us a complex reading of land that shifts the ground beneath our feet. The differences expressed through stitch and line, as we scan across the cloth, are as immense as the skills deployed by hundreds of members of the Embroiderers' Guild of Australia. The embroidery opens up a plethora of questions around nationhood and identity that challenges ideological assumptions held by many European settlers as to who "owns" the land. A struggle as to what constitutes "Australian" identity is vividly articulated as the complexities of history are pushed to the very edges of visual and material representation. The negotiations between Lawrence and the embroiderers offer insight into the tensions of spatial communication and community networks that are distinct from the virtual ebb and flow of real time exchanges through the pixel patchwork screen.

Victoria Lynn's analysis of Mrinalini Mukherjee's monumental sculptures executed in vegetable fiber in "India Inside-Out", provoke further questions as to what is interpreted as art or craft and by whom. First shown in England, at

Textile, Volume 1, Issue 2, pp. 115–117
Reprints available directly from the Publishers.
Photocopying permitted by licence only.
© 2003 Berg. Printed in the United Kingdom.

the Museum of Modern Art in Oxford in 1994, Lynn interprets Mukherjee's work through a critical engagement with the catalog texts that pre-suppose a pre-technological way of knowing the world. As Lynn argues, Mukherjee's practice frustrates the notion that modernism, craft and a fascination with ancient sculptural and architectural forms should be seen as mutually exclusive. No singular reading will suffice. The work can be "read" through the influences on Mukherjee's youth at art school in India: Indian modernism, Tagore's philosophy, Subranmanyan's embracement of craft, a belief in nature and a love of nature. Such inter-textual reading brings a diversity of histories into an overlapping, intertwined visual and contemporary experience. No single knot suffices, only an accumulation of the many that build an extraordinary self-portrait—an abundant exuberance that folds in on itself as it twists and turns through shifting modularities of form. References to Deleuze's writing on the fold offer a route through Mukherjee's work. In "Chinese Whispers: Variations on Textile," Ros Gray takes up this proposition as a way of under-standing textile as a textured surface upon which subjects come into being from different points of view. In a riveting series of moves across the cinematic frame of the remarkable film, *Ju Dou*, the meaning of textile twists and turns.

It folds and is shaped via a nuanc attention to texture, textuality and tissue, form and tone that immers us in stories of cloth and clothmaking. In a series of subtle shifts, cloth and clothmaking are further evoked through Piranesi's scenographies, Watteau's *Voyage Cythera* and Vivienne Westwood's fashion collections. At one and the same moment, questions as to the use and abuse of craft and labor a mobilized. The appearance of subjectivity comes into play, as a to be thought of entity.

The notion of the textile and it relation to the cinematic screen is expanded. The computer screen relays new forms of art works. Bot offer new ways of imagining new subjectivities, readings and practices in which disparate voice interact and intersect among a network of spaces, texts and pattern. The essays in issue 2, together with the visionary and personal poem "The Warp of my Life" interleave wefts dyed with dreams. What have they in common? Each essay begins to dissolve the fixed categories of wl we think of as art or craft, cloth ar labor, objective and subjective realities, time and space as the ve idea of old identities are transformed and re-made.

Janis Jeffe
on behalf of co-edit
Pennina Barnett and Doran R

Pixel Patchwork: "Quilting in Time" Online

```
###########################################################################
# ,,,   ###############        {~}        ###############        ,
#{{{}}}#######  {~} {~}      ~Y~      {~} {~}  ######{{{
# ~Y~  #####  ~Y~ ~Y~  #######  ~Y~ ~Y~    #####  ~Y
# \|/  ##############################################  \|
# ,,,  #    #    #    #    #    #    #    #    #    ,
#{{{}}}#    #    #    #    #    #    #    # m #    #{{{
# ~Y~  # b # T #    #    #    #  S # r #    #  ~Y
# \|/  # r # a # D # d # R # S # t # t # j # \|
# ,,,  # a # c # e # o # o # h # A # | # a #  ,
#{{{}}}# t # k # b # r # d # e # r # a # m #{{{
# ~Y~  # - # ` # b # e # n # r # B # w # m #  ~Y
# \|/  # a # A # i # m # e # ^ # r # a # e #  \|
# ,,,  # f # F # W # i # y #    # B # y # r #  ,
#{{{}}}# k # K #    #    #    #    #    # | #  #{{{
# ~Y~  #    #    #    #    #    #    #    #    #  ~Y
# \|/  #    #    #    #    #    #    #    #    #  \|
# ,,,  ###############################################  ,
#{{{}}}#    {~} {~}  ###### {~} {~}  ######{{{
# ~Y~  ######  ~Ï~ ~Ï~  {~}  ~Ï~ ~Ï~  ######  ~Y
# \|/  ###############  ~Ï~    ###############  \|
###########################################################################
```

Abstract

"Text" and "textile" share the same Latin root—*textus*, or "woven." In the 1960s and 1970s a digital form of amateur text-based art known as "ASCII (pronounced *AS-kee*) art" began to flourish— images created with letters and other typographic symbols on the computer keyboard. Since the advent of Windows 95, participants in certain "channels" (chatrooms) on IRC (Internet Relay Chat) have developed a brilliantly colored form of text-based art, an elaboration of ASCII art. This art contains much play with ornament, pattern, and symmetry, and may be either abstract or figurative. In a highly ritualized mode of playful communication, images are displayed on the screen in real time to greet other participants. Thus, images are both "art" and "communication." Despite its intangibility, this art has many affinities with traditional weaving, embroidery and especially quilting. It is a form of "quilting in time" rather than space. Figurative images also partially resemble paper greeting cards. This article focuses on an IRC group called *"rainbow,"* that has communicated mainly via images since May 1997. The analysis draws on a database of some 5,000 images. Seven distinctive features of this art are discussed.

BRENDA DANET

Brenda Danet is Professor Emerita of Sociology and Communication at the Hebrew University of Jerusalem, and a visiting fellow in Sociology, Yale University, 2000–2003. She has been studying communication and culture on the Internet since 1991, and is the author of *Cyberpl@y: Communicating online* (Berg Publishers, Oxford, 2001, distributed in the United States by New York University Press; companion Website, http://atar.mscc.huji.ac.il/~msdanet/cyberpl@y/). Her current research combines interests in online communication with concerns in folk art, material culture, the aesthetics of everyday life, and the anthropology of art and ritual.

Textile, Volume 1, Issue 2, pp. 118–143
Reprints available directly from the Publishers.
Photocopying permitted by licence only.
© 2003 Berg. Printed in the United Kingdom.

Pixel Patchwork: "Quilting in Time" Online

This article is about a novel form of online visual expression that I call "*pixel patchwork*."[1] Instead of typing words, as is usual in verbal chat, participants in certain "channels" or chatrooms on IRC (Internet Relay Chat), one of the world's most popular online chat modes, interact primarily via the display of brilliantly colored images created with letters and other typographic symbols on the computer keyboard. Text-based images have been featured on a number of IRC channels since 1996–7, but have particularly flourished on #*mirc_rainbow*, *rainbow* for short, a channel on the Undernet, a major network of IRC servers.[2] "*mIRC*" is the Windows-based program players use to communicate and display images.[3]

Participants engage in everyday, spontaneous communication via images, and also hold scheduled events such as art shows, channel anniversary celebrations, and birthday parties, again primarily featuring images rather than words. Though dependent on Windows 95+ and in some respects on rather advanced computer literacy, artists employ very simple, even "primitive" digital techniques, when compared with cutting-edge computer graphics.[4] Borrowing a term from world music, I call this art "*avant-folk*," because it strikingly juxtaposes considerable skill using computers with naive, group-based artistic expression resembling traditional folk art in important

respects—despite two main, apparent anomalies, the lack of tangibility and of face-to-face contact between participants. "Folk-like" aspects of the art will be debated in the concluding section of the article.

Figure 1 is an excellent introduction to *rainbow* art and communication. As is typical of many forms of online chat, the players use nicknames, called "nicks" on IRC. Three players have deployed five different images to greet one another. The nick of each player appears at the left of each line of an image, just as if a person typed ordinary text.

First, ‹rebel^›, a Texas housewife and web page designer, greets me as I enter the channel—my nick is ‹doremi›.[5] Next, ‹Steakie^›, a male signage installer from Pennsylvania, greets ‹swt1^› and ‹aisa›, who types "hello" followed by eight inverted exclamation points, giving away her Spanish origins. Then ‹swt1^› acknowledges ‹Steakie›, who greets her a second time, adding the words, "how ya been?" All have mobilized ready-made files from collections stored on their hard disks, incorporating the recipient's nick just before displaying them.

Visual images composed from the elements of writing have a long history. Antecedents include pattern, concrete or visual poetry, Islamic calligraphy, micrography, typewriter art, and teletype art.[6] The most recent antecedent is ASCII (*AS-kee*) art—images created using e basic typographic characters on e computer keyboard.[7] Since the ‚60s and 1970s, programmers, ‚ckers, and other mostly male ‚mputer professionals have been ‚ating images from letters, ‚mbers, and other typographic ‚mbols. By the 1990s, people of all ‚lks of life, all ages, women as ‚ll as men, were collecting and ‚ating ASCII art.

IRC art is an elaboration of ASCII art. This is most apparent when IRC art is figurative: three images in Figure 1 contain adaptations of ASCII art creations by Joan Stark, an Ohio housewife and mother, and a popular artist whose works are often adapted for IRC. The representation of lightning in the first image, the small angels in the second, and the cartoon-like image

of "Nessie," the Loch Ness monster, in the third are all originally designed by her. ‹sher^› adapted the lightning and monster motifs for IRC (and also designed the last "HI" image).

Interaction on *rainbow* can be puzzling to the casual observer. Participants spend hours and hours in the channel, day after day, even year after year, endlessly greeting

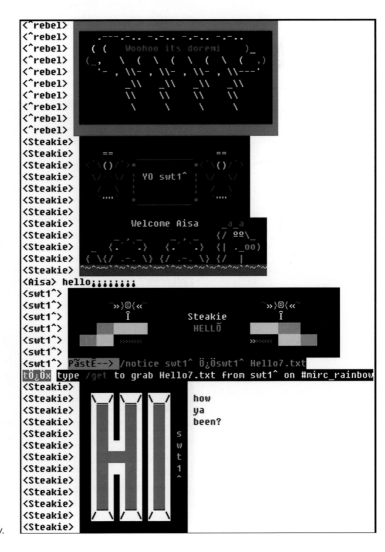

and acknowledging one another via images, never saying much in the conventional sense. Usually, there is not even much small talk. What, then, can be the fascination? Surely, the sheer novelty of the phenomenon must wear off.

The goal of this article is to identify the distinctive features of this novel art, and to explain how it also serves as a language of communication. I will attempt to do so in a manner comprehensible to readers not necessarily familiar with the Internet or with this specific phenomenon. I aspire both to identify affinities with traditional, material-based arts and crafts, and to illuminate novel aspects of this digital phenomenon. My descriptions and analyses draw on a database of approximately 5,000 images captured and saved over a period of five and a half years, using Paint Shop Pro, a graphics program.[8] In the conclusion to the article I will allude to some of the directions that my analysis of this art and communication have taken. In addition, I will attempt to make a case for viewing this art as an incipient form of digital folk art.

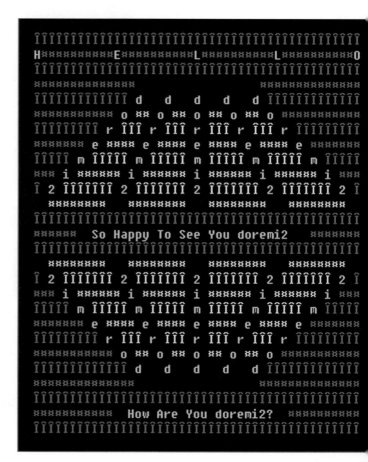

Figure 2
An abstract image by <nuffers>.

troduction

ne words "text," "texture," and extile" all have the same root—the tin *textus*, "woven." While carpets e usually knotted or woven from e bottom up, this digital art is voven" from the top down, left to ght, as in knitting and ordinary ord-processing. When creating an C image, one "knits" each "stitch" m left to right, determining nether it will contain a typographic mbol or not, what color it will be,

and what color the background will be. While shortcuts of various kinds can be used to make the process less tedious, the fundamental process remains the same.

Types of rainbow *art and links to traditional folk art*

Rainbow art may be either abstract or figurative; both are about equally common. In abstract images, typographic symbols are typically repeated in patterned ways, though

not always as elaborately as in Figure 2. Figurative images are "drawn" with typographic symbols, either in so-called "solid style" (Figure 3), or "line style" (Figure 4), as has been true also of ASCII art.

While abstract images are almost without exception original works by IRC artists, many, perhaps most figurative images incorporate and adapt works taken from ASCII art collections on the web, as in the instances noted in Figure 1, and as

gure 3

figurative image by <jazzman>, corporating an ASCII rose by Normand eilleux, http://www.afn.org/~afn39695/ eilleux.htm.

is also the case for the rose in Figure 3, originally by Normand Veilleux.[9] The arrangement of cats in Figure 4 is again based on a design of a single cat by Joan Stark, but now transformed considerably because of the carefully planned repetitions of the basic design element.[10]

These examples suggest that figurative images are generally two-dimensional, non-illusionistic, stylized, seemingly frozen in time and space, like those in many types of traditional folk art. Similarly, abstract designs often resemble geometric designs in carpets, weavings, cross-stitch embroidery, needlepoint, and patchwork quilts.[11] *Rainbow* images resemble works in these crafts primarily because they too are created on a grid, not necessarily visible to the eye.

From material to digital quilting

Rainbow art is a form of "quilting in time," rather than space, in which the "patches" consist only of bits and bytes. The display of images in social context partially resembles traditional North American quilting bees, in which women met not only to combine the layers of a quilt, but also to socialize. The women chatted while working, and after the quilting the men joined them for socializing and dancing (Dewhurst *et al.* 1979: 51–2; Yabsley 1984: 56). While social aspects of quilting were certainly important, traditional quilts were primarily functional domestic objects in poor homes, made from scraps of old clothing to keep people warm as bedcovers.

Rainbow images do not have such utilitarian functions. However,

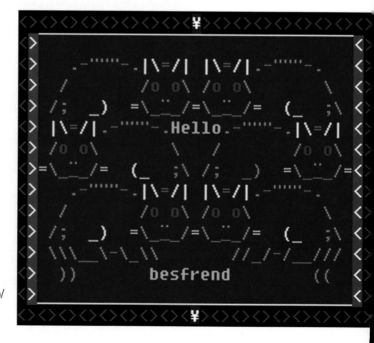

Figure 4
A stylized figurative image by <dale^>, adapted from an ASCII design by Joan Stark, http://web.archive.org/web/20010411185704/www.geocities.com/SoHo/7373/pets.htm.

splays of images do serve an portant function of a different nd: they facilitate the cultivation group ties, not just in a brief, heduled event, as is true of iltings, but over an extended riod of time—weeks, months, en years. Behind the façade of oup activity, I have learned, many dividuals come to cultivate private lationships, in two-party online nversations, parallel to the oup's channel and not visible to hers, and in subsidiary channels e players have created. These clude a second channel where

some players go to receive technical help, to rehearse displays, and to chat in verbal text mode. There is poignancy in this form of online quilting: whereas a cloth quilt persists over time, long after the social relationships surrounding its creation and use no longer exist, this art is entirely ephemeral— just how ephemeral is explained below.

Despite the analogy to quilting, *rainbow* players do not use terms associated with it. They speak of "coloring" and "drawing" "art," in rather child-like fashion. Still, the

analogy is salient for some. A woman nicknamed ‹patches› was webmistress for the channel website and channel "owner" or leader from 1999 to 2002. As her nickname hints, she is an experienced quilter, who claims to have sold commissioned quilts for thousands of dollars. In a private chat in 1997 I asked her if she saw a resemblance between IRC art and quilting. She immediately displayed for me three quilt patterns she had transformed into IRC images. One of these, "Trip Around the World," is shown in Figure 5.

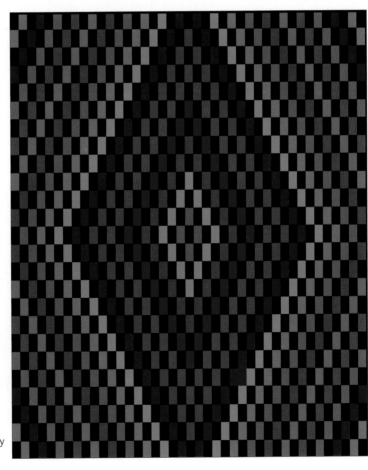

Figure 5
"Trip Around the World," an IRC version of a traditional American quilt pattern, by ‹patches›.

Social History of rainbow

Rainbow came into existence in May 1997, when, unhappy about the autocratic and tension-laden atmosphere in another Undernet channel featuring images and called "*#mirc_colors*," three members defected to create a new channel with a more egalitarian, freer atmosphere. Since then, *rainbow* has flourished, despite quite high turnover among participants. A fairly stable core of regulars and a well-organized set of ongoing artistic and social practices have crystallized. Hundreds of people have participated over the years, though just how many is impossible to determine. Some drop in just once, never to return; others participate regularly for months and even years at a time. At the present time, some seventy-five individuals are members of the "in-group," serving as "ops," operators in IRC lingo—participants with administrative duties and privileges, who help run the channel. Many are also artists.

I estimate that, over time, some 150 artists have contributed to the pool of images shared by all. Non-artists regularly use images created by others as "tokens for interaction." Some sets of images are devoted to the work of individual artists. In these instances, the work of a single artist is honored in a scheduled show, and then the file is immediately released for all to use in ordinary interaction.

Other sets of files combine the work of many different artists, grouped by theme, such as "winterfun," "Christmas," or "jokes." These files, too, are shared by all. On 30 December 2002 there were no less than 248 sets of files available for downloading from the channel website, the large majority of which had been created by *rainbow* artists. If one estimates 10 images per set (too low in my experience, in many instances), this is an output of some 25,000 images.

The players are of lower-middle class to lower-class background, and generally have had some high school education, or are high-school graduates; some have post-high-school vocational training. Few are professionals. About 60% are women and 40% men; most are in their thirties, forties, and fifties, though there are also teenagers and people in their sixties and seventies. Most are Americans concentrated in the West, Southwest, and South, with a smattering of people from many other countries. Some channel leaders have had higher levels of education than rank-and-file players. ‹sher^›, the current leader, is a housewife married to a coal miner. Not surprisingly, a fair number of artists have previous experience with materially based crafts such as quilting, sewing, and embroidery. I know of only one professionally trained artist with an MFA among currently active artists.

Features of *Rainbow* Art

I turn now to a discussion of seven distinctive features of *rainbow* art (Figure 6).

Interactivity

The first, fundamental feature of this art listed in Figure 6 is *interactivity*. This term means many things to many people.[12] Here, it

ure 6
en features of *rainbow* art.

1. Interactivity
2. Ephemerality
3. Use of brilliant color
4. Sound clips: trend toward multimedia performance
5. Prominence of ornament, pattern, and symmetry
6. Eccentric typography: extended ASCII characters
7. Prefabricated utterances in figurative images

ans that people interact directly h other people in real time, and t just with computers or with web ges. This contrasts sharply with o other online "quilting" enomena, both on the World de Web.

Since approximately 2001, rital "friendship quilts," web-sed assemblages of "patches" ntributed by various individuals, nerally women, can be found on e web. They are an adaptation of e idea of traditional American endship quilts, which were "made of a one-block pattern repeated oughout the entire quilt . . . ny, or all, of the blocks in a quilt ve names on them, either cribed in ink or embroidered in k thread or cotton floss" (Lipsett 97: 16).[13] Friends and relatives ch contributed a block with their mes on them.

Figure 7 is an excellent example a traditional friendship quilt. de about 1888 in Cayuga County, state New York, it was presented Reverend Cordello C. Herrick and wife Emily Elizabeth Taylor rrick. It now hangs in the family om of Brian Wells Galusha and his fe, the great-granddaughter of s couple.[14]

The size of the patches in digital endship quilts (Figure 8)

crystallized at 130 × 130 pixels, perfect squares. Typically, there are four or five patches in a row, and five or more rows. Many patches are *live*: clicking on them leads directly to the website of the person contributing them. Some are also animated. Patches are usually figurative, greeting-card-like in imagery and accompanying mini-texts, as in Figure 8, the upper portion of a digital friendship quilt by Suzie Radant, a Michigan resident, who calls her site "Suzie's Cyber Cloud Quilts: Quilts with Meaning."

Most digital quilters offer downloadable patches to others. Sharing is a way of being in touch with others and making friends. The links between sites constitute a social network of sorts, and some sites are organized into webrings. Suzie Radant manages a webring called "Quilting Circle of Friends." Compared to *rainbow*, whose participants interact in real time, social ties among these digital quilters seem weak, and are, at the least, invisible to the casual visitor to their sites.[15]

Another, very different subculture of digital quilting, online since November 2000, is a branch of the computer underground art scene, located at Tiles.ice.org. Until

recently, the iconography of these mainly male groups of teenagers and young adults was lurid, transgressive, often violent, drawing on comics, science fiction, horror films, and other elements in popular culture. While these trends are still in evidence, changes are also afoot. Surprisingly, some artists are now creating large, generally surrealistic images they too call "quilts."[16] Participants work on "tiles"—their term for patches—of huge figurative, high-resolution images, done by individuals who do not know much about what is adjacent. Jon Shirin, *aka* "slothy," the enterprising promoter of this form of amateur art and manager of the site, writes:

Tiles.ice.org is iCE's answer to the old-fashioned quilt party, minus the gathering of elderly women. It's a unique opportunity for collaborative [sic] artwork on the net. A huge image, composed of individual 'tiles' is created, one piece at a time. The goal when making a tile is to mesh your work as smoothly as possible with the surrounding tiles, while creating something cool, artistic, and if applicable, on-topic.

Figure 7
A traditional American friendship quilt,
presented to Reverend Cordello C.
Herrick and his wife Emily Elizabeth
Taylor Herrick, Cayuga County, upstate
New York, *c.* 1888 (full view, detail).
http://www.rootsweb.com/~nycayuga/
quilt/#quilt. Photos courtesy of
Brian Wells Galusha.

ure 8
per portion of a digital friendship quilt
Suzie Radant, "Suzie's Cyber Cloud
lts: Quilts with Meaning," http://
ieque.net/friendshipquilt.htm.

ticipation resembles working
gether on a giant puzzle—but in
s case *creating* it, not putting
own parts together. Artists are
en just a fifteen-pixel border of
acent material, so they can align
ir creation with the rest of the
sign. "Signing out" a given tile,
y must complete it in twenty-four
urs; if not, it becomes available to
ers. Holding the cursor over
se works, visitors can
nporarily reveal information
out the creators of individual
s.

A quilt in progress as of January
2002 (Figure 9) was called "Knots."
Knots and ropes of endless varieties
of texture, color and shape were
"braided" together. Participants in
these digital quilts are primarily
creating collective artworks, not
cultivating social ties or expressing
group solidarity, as I shall argue is
the case for *rainbow* players,
although they do tend to think of
themselves as a community.
Revisiting the site in January 2003, I
learned that "Knots" was one of no
less than ninety-seven completed

quilts. Twenty-two individuals had
contributed to it.[17]

Ephemerality

A second distinctive feature of
rainbow art (Figure 6) is that it is
truly *ephemeral*, even more so than
ASCII art, even though both consist
of bits and bytes. Whereas ASCII art
can be viewed offline on a computer
in any text-editing program,
ordinarily *rainbow* art can be viewed
only when (1) one is logged on to
the Internet; (2) the *mIRC* program is
open; (3) one has connected

Figure 9
"Knots," detail from a computer underground "quilt" in progress, January 2002. http://Tiles.ice.org.

successfully to an IRC server; and (4) one has joined a channel.[18] Also, while one can print ASCII art, IRC images can be printed only if they are first transformed into regular graphic images, as I have done, both in my research generally, and in the case of all illustrations for this article. Similarly, IRC images must be transformed into graphic images for display on the web.

Brilliant color

Another important characteristic of IRC art is the burst into brilliant color, not visible in the print version of the illustrations for this article. Its predecessor, ASCII art, is usually shown white on black, or black on a white background. On early computer screens it was displayed in phosphorescent green or amber pixels on a dark screen.

The sixteen colors that may be used in *mIRC*, as in any Windows-based program, include the three primary colors, red, yellow, and blue, as well many other shades, along with black, gray, and white. One can choose the color both of the typographic symbol in a given "slot" in an image and of its background. One can also create images consisting of just solid colors, though this is much rarer. Although one cannot mix colors, w careful control of adjacent colors one can create three-dimensional effects, and modify the appearanc of a given color. The diamond-shaped image in Figure 10 appear to have depth because of the controlled use of black, blue-black bright blue, gray, and white. The effect resembles some 1960s Op A (Parola 1996).

The players' love of bright color
ometimes quite explicit. One
ge included the mini-text, "Hey!
k! They've added colors to this
ck and white world." Love for the
taposition of many bright colors
lso reflected in the channel
ne, *rainbow*.
What Hans and Shulamith
itler have written about the love
color characterizes *rainbow*
yers too:

*he love of color is especially
rominent in childhood and in
re-literate societies, as well as
adults who undergo a
osening of conscious control
ue to autism, regression, or
sychosis or to a poisonous
elirium or a drug-induced*

*intoxication . . . color [is] a factor
appealing to the deeper
nonrational layers of personality.*
(Kreitler and Kreitler 1972: 54–5)

Especially when alternated, gaudy
colors are perceived to ward off evil
in many cultures (Paine 1990: 148).
    David Batchelor (2001: 31–2)
notes that there is an old
relationship between drugs and
color. Aristotle "called color a
drug—*pharmakon* . . . to . . . Plato
. . . a painter was merely 'a grinder
and mixer of multi-colour drugs'"
(Batchelor 2001), citing Lichtenstein
(1993: 54) and Riley (1995: 20). Of
more recent times, Batchelor notes:

*During the 1960s . . . drugs were
commonly . . . associated . . .*

*with the intensification of
colour . . . Think of psychedelia;
think of the album covers, the
posters, the lyrics . . .
—Ecstasy . . . is the name given
to a widely used psychotropic
stimulant, but it is also a
synonym for Roland Barthes'
remarkable description of
colour . . . Bliss, jouissance,
ecstasy . . . "Colour . . . is a kind
of bliss . . . like a closing eyelid,
a tiny fainting spell."* (Batchelor
2001: 31–2)

The color red is particularly
prominent in *rainbow* imagery of
both figurative and abstract kinds,
not just in images conventionally
associated with Christmas,
Valentine's Day, or the Fourth of

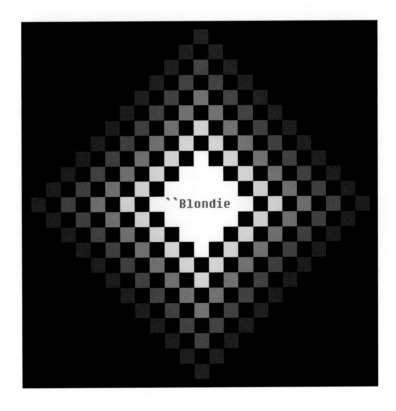

ure 10
hree-dimensional design by
ghtrose>.

July, but in everyday ones too. The Kreitlers (1972: 69) suggest that red is "the most meaning-laden color," carrying associations both to life and birth and to danger and death. "More than any other, the color red is perceived as a carrier of force" (Varichon, 2000: 69; my translation). In many cultures it is associated with magic and ritual (Hibi 2000; Varichon 2000). Sheila Paine sums up many of these themes:

> Red is the most powerful, the most vibrant, the most exhilarating of colors; it is the blood of life and of death . . . it is also ambiguous: life, fire, the sun and power are counterbalanced by sacrifice and death. Red threads and fabrics are associated with spirit worship and demons, with youth and marriage, with talismanic charms and secret powers. It is the predominant colour in all tribal and peasant embroidery, but is used in two entirely different ways—to protect and to mark. (Paine 1990: 148)

Black is also very prominent in *rainbow* art, primarily as filled background, for both abstract and figurative images. While the Kreitlers summarize research indicating that black "implies death, night, anxiety, defeat, and depression" (Kreitler and Kreitler 1972: 69), it is also often associated with magic and mystery. This association is relevant here too, as in the black of the darkened theater enhancing the magic of a performance. Black helps to conjure up a protected, magical space, set off from the potentially ominous messiness of the physical world. More pragmatically, a black background also contrasts well with the use of bright colors; when images are backlit on the computer screen, the colors seem to glow.

Sound clips: the trend toward multimedia performance

Fourth, *rainbow* images are often displayed together with a brief sound clip, either of songs or, less commonly, of real-life sounds such as something crashing, or laughter. The players create and collect sounds, to a lesser extent than they create and collect images. Many scheduled shows have sets of sound files to go with them. Players must download and install the sound files in advance. Only if sounds are already on players' hard disks will they be able to hear them when activated in context. A special genre developed for shows is "timed texts," extended sequences of large images accompanied by longer sound clips, even whole songs.

Prominence of ornament, pattern, and symmetry

Fifth, and perhaps most important for my research agenda, *rainbow* features prominent ornament, pattern, and symmetry, as is abundantly clear in Figures 2 and James Trilling (2001: 6) defines ornament as "the elaboration of functionally complete objects for the sake of visual pleasure." The *Grove Dictionary of Art* offers a broader definition; ornament and pattern are:

> decorative devices applied or incorporated as embellishment.

[They] are not generally essential *... the structure of an object, but* *they can . . . emphasize or* *disguise structural elements, particularly in architecture, and they can fulfil an iconographic role . . .[19]*

The creation of pattern relies on three characteristics, a unit, repetition of that unit, and a system organization.

A pattern can be defined as a design composed of one or more motifs, multiplied and arranged in an orderly sequence, and a single motif as a unit with which the designer composes a pattern by repeating it at regular intervals over a surface. The motif itself is not a pattern, but it is used to create patterns. (Phillips and Bunce 1993: 7)

In theory, *rainbow* players could create images consisting just of one block of solid color, inserting the recipient's nick before displaying them. In terms of communicative function narrowly construed, such "plain" images would be adequate. In fact, participants never play such images. *In five and a half years of following the channel, I have never seen a single image without either a figurative component or some play with color or typography or both, creating some kind of pattern or symmetry.*

"Symmetry . . . is one idea by which man through the ages has tried to comprehend and create order, beauty, and perfection" (Weyl 1952: 5). It pertains to "the correspondence in size, form and arrangement of parts on opposite sides of a plane, line, or point," or to "regularity of form or

arrangement with reference to corresponding parts."[20] My analyses suggest that the turn to pattern and symmetry in *rainbow* art has deep psychological and social roots, and that vertical bilateral symmetry in particular serves as a visual metaphor for *communitas* (Pocius 1979; Danet in preparation).

It is intriguing that there is little evidence of concern with pattern and symmetry in the earlier ASCII art, which is almost entirely figurative. In contrast, pattern and symmetry abound in *rainbow* art, not only in all-over abstract designs like Figure 2, but also in the fields of figurative designs (Figure 4),[21] and particularly in the borders surrounding many images, whether abstract or figurative. In Figure 11 the border is especially elaborate, far more so, in fact, than the field.

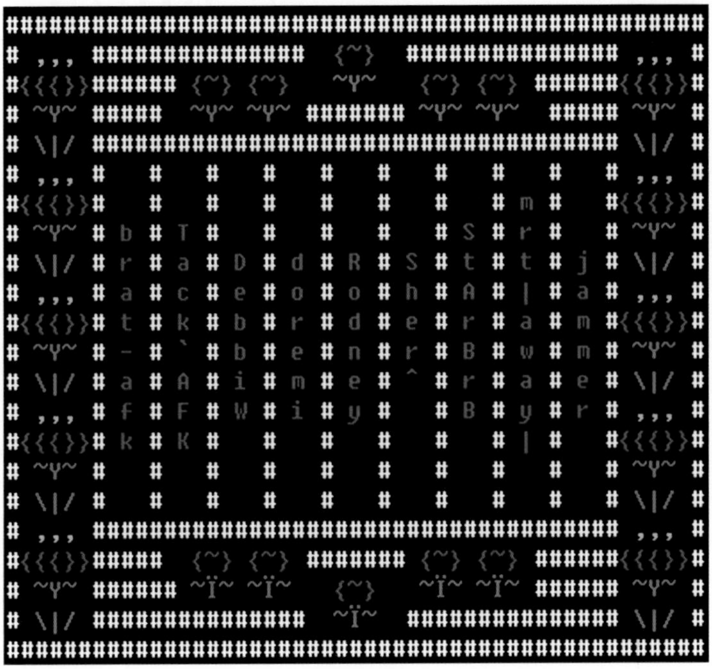

Figure 11

Pattern and symmetry in the border of a "Multiple," by <sher^>.

This is an example of a "multiple," a subgenre of images the players developed in which it is possible to honor or acknowledge two or more individuals by nick at the same time. Here, nine players are honored, including me.

Eccentric typography: extended ASCII characters

Very frequently, pattern and symmetry feature unfamiliar, so-called extended ASCII characters, in Figure 2, typographic symbols that require eight bits to code the

Figure 12
A selection of extended ASCII characters and their codes.

t seven. Therefore they are not ed in plain text such as e-mail. mbols such as the Japanese Yen n ¥ and the š of Slavic languages appreciated for their interesting phic shapes and potential as sign elements, both within image lds and in borders.

Figure 12 displays some ended ASCII characters with the des for creating them manually. can see that systematic etition creates interesting visual tterns. Evidently, because many nbols are exotic to artists, mostly tive English speakers, they can re easily pay attention to their phic possibilities than if symbols very familiar. Symbols from eryday English usage not used in in text are also popular, :luding the British £ symbol, as ll as those for "copyright" and egistered"—© and ®. In Figure 2 ich sense of texture was created

with just two extended ASCII symbols.

Occasionally, *rainbow* artists also use exotic typographic symbols to enhance the words in short texts; they call this practice the use of "fancy letters." Originally, it was hackers who used eccentric typographic characters in plain text, intentionally reducing legibility. They did so in order to annoy, to be outrageous and transgressive, and to signal membership in an elitist in-group. It is ironic that IRC players have domesticated and democratized this practice. For them, eccentric typography in meaningful verbal texts is merely decorative and ceremonial.

Pre-fabricated utterances in figurative images

A final distinctive feature of *rainbow* art is the inclusion of a short text in

figurative images, as in traditional paper greeting cards. The mini-text in Figure 3 is typical: "I searched the world for a perfect rose . . . I found you . . . perfect as a rose." *Rainbow* artists no doubt draw on their experience with paper greeting cards when designing figurative works and composing the mini-texts to go with them. These mini-texts transform images from "just art" into usable potential tokens for interaction. They are a variety of "pre-fabricated utterances" (Herrnstein-Smith 1978: 59), verbal structures pre-assembled for later use as natural utterances. The function of a greeting-card message is "not to *represent* a natural utterance but to *become* one" (Herrnstein-Smith 1978: 60).

Some mini-texts are sentimental, like the one in Figure 3; others are humorous and light-hearted, like the punning example

jure 13
numorous figurative image, by <glint>, apted from a work by Joan Stark, :p://web.archive.org/web/ 010411185704/www.geocities.com/ Ho/7373/pets.htm.

in Figure 13: "Hey there . . . did you hear? Fedex and UPS are buying out the US Postal Service . . . They are going to call it 'FEDUP.'" Some are metaphoric or non-executable in nature, as in the invitation, "Sail away with me," combined with an image of a sailboat. This mixture of serious, even sentimental elements and humorous ones points to the hybrid nature of *rainbow* art and communication as paradoxically both mock and serious.[22]

Discussion

This overview of *rainbow* art has shown that it shares many features with traditional arts and crafts, yet in other respects is a unique digital, online phenomenon. The most novel features are its intangibility and ephemerality, and its role as a language of communication in real time, among people who mostly have never met in the physical world.

Appropriation versus creativity

I have noted that *rainbow* artists frequently appropriate ASCII works from collections on the web when designing figurative images. Therefore, some might conclude that there is little creativity in the figurative varieties of this art. They might claim that all artists are doing is recoding and coloring images for use on IRC—mere technical exercises. On the contrary, I would argue, there is considerable creativity in choosing an image, determining a demarcated space for it and locating it in that space,[23] choosing the colors to be used, designing a complementary border, often with some of the same, or at least coordinated colors, and

preparing a suitable mini-text to bring it to life as a potential communicative act, as in Figures 3 and 13.

Some artists specialize in creating figurative images. Others are very skilled in creating original pleasing patterns and types of symmetry, including some that are difficult to execute in this medium. Indeed, the artists enjoy the challenge of creating ever-new and striking effects and genres of images, pushing this very restricted medium to its limits.

Striving for good gestalts

This article has been primarily descriptive. In further work on *rainbow* art, only hinted at here, I examine evidence for the hypothesis that creating, playing, and viewing images are all means for the players to strive for a sense of closure, completion, or perfection—in other words, for "good gestalts"—for forms that are characterized by "regularity, symmetry, inclusiveness, unity, harmony, maximal simplicity, and conciseness" (Kreitler and Kreitler 1972: 83). The notion of gestalt pertains to our tendency to perceive a stimulus as "whole" even if some portion of it is absent, or to prefer "wholes" to stimuli that are less than whole. A basic assumption of gestalt theory is that people naturally strive for good gestalts, for stimuli that are organized. The theory contends that unorganized stimuli are experienced as tension producing, whereas organized stimuli are experienced as tension reducing. [24]

Thinking primarily of primitive ethnographic art, Hans and Shulamith Kreitler noted that:

*he art of primitive peoples
*onsists mainly of good gestalts,
*haracterized by simplicity,
losure, regularity and symmetry
. . it is this function of the visual
*rts—the presentation of good
*estalts—which lends meaning
*o the image of the artist as a
*od or magician who lures order
*ut of chaos and vanquishes the
*ormless by forms. (Kreitler and
*reitler 1972: 91–2; emphasis
dded)

r research suggests that *rainbow*
*rticipants have a strong need for
osure, for good gestalts.

  Because the pursuit of closure in
nbow art occurs in a social
*ntext, I believe that formal
*pects of images are not just of
*ychological significance, but also
*ve important connections with
e social nature of communication
*line. That is, a case can be made
at creating, playing, and viewing
ages with certain formal
*aracteristics are also a means to
*ive for *enclosure*—for a sense of
longing, for *communitas* (Turner
*69, 1974). In this context, the
*nnection between the terms
losure" and "enclosure" is not
*erely eytomological, but
*npirical. The many forms of
*petition in images serve as
*etaphors for togetherness.
*deed, one could almost reduce
is thesis to a formula:

*Visual) twoness = (social)
ogetherness.

  One striking type of evidence for
e claim that *rainbow* artists and
ayers strive for good gestalts
rtains to emergent norms about
e use of ASCII art in their work,
and acceptable forms of credit for
accomplishment. Surprisingly, most
rainbow artists embed the name,
initials or nickname of the ASCII
artist whose work has been
appropriated, along with their own
nick, in the hidden coding of the
image, making credit for the artists
invisible when the image is
displayed online in full color. Those
"in the know" are aware that hidden
initials, nicks, or names of artists
may be viewed (generally after the
fact) in black and white channel
logs, or, more conveniently, when
one sweeps the cursor briefly over
an image currently displayed. This
depletes the image of color
temporarily and reveals hidden
material. However, those not aware
of these options would never learn
the identities of artists via either of
them.[25]

  Obviously, this practice is
radically different from the
convention of the artist's signature
on a work, which overtly claims
credit for achievement, and asserts
intellectual property rights
regarding its disposition. In a query
addressed to *rainbow* ops and
artists on their Yahoo group forum, I
asked if this practice did not deprive
artists of full credit. To my great
surprise, several artists replied that
making names and initials visible
would spoil the image: thus,
creating and viewing good gestalts
are, evidently, more important to
them than intellectual property
rights.

  Avoiding extraneous material
that would "spoil" an image is just
one of eight strategies that I have
identified that players and artists
use in pursuit of good gestalts.
Unfortunately, for lack of space,
details of other strategies and
accompanying examples could not
be included here, except for several
hints that the concern with pattern
and symmetry is critical.[26] Contrary
to Trilling's (2001) view of ornament
as nonfunctional embellishment
purely for visual pleasure,
ornament, pattern, and symmetry—
along with certain aspects of the
iconography of figurative images—
are not merely decorative. Rather,
they reflect and express profound
psychological and social needs and
aspirations among *rainbow* players
and artists.

Rainbow art as digital folk art

As suggested at the beginning of
this article, I believe that *rainbow*
art may be viewed as an incipient
form of digital folk art. On the face
of it, several glaringly anomalous
aspects of this art make such a
claim seem foolhardy.

  First, the art is hardly
"traditional," since it has been in
existence only since the advent of
Windows 95 and the Windows
version of the IRC software. In
contrast, for folklorists, tradition
involves entire generations of
individuals, families, groups,
handing down certain practices,
and, no less important, primarily in
face-to-face interaction. Most
rainbow participants, on the other
hand, have never met in the
physical world. Moreover, as
mentioned earlier, there has been
considerable turnover among the
players, despite a devoted core of
regulars.

  Finally, unlike traditional folk art
as we know it today, there is no
market for this art, which circulates
in a gift economy, rather than one
based on money. Not monetary
value, but reputation among the

players and other artists, within the group and on IRC generally, and the aesthetic satisfactions of creating the art are what motivates artists.

Despite these anomalies, two main features of this art justify viewing it as a form of digital folk art, in my opinion. Contemporary formulations of the field of folklore make these anomalies far less glaring than they appear on first sight. Henry Glassie has written, "Today we think of folklore not as a kind of material but as a kind of *action*" (Glassie 1989: 34, italics added). A particularly influential definition is that of Dan Ben Amos, for whom folklore is "artistic communication in small groups" (Ben Amos 1971). While the focus on this definition is on communication, the smallness of the group is certainly a potential issue in the present context.

Rainbow players can be said to be creating an instant tradition. It *is* unsettling that the Internet speeds up social processes that in the past we expected to take years, decades, generations. Despite the turnover among participants to which I have alluded, there are remarkable continuities over the last five years in channel practices. Moreover, the players have domesticated the medium of computer text art, formerly the domain of transgressive hackers, in a manner that reinforces traditional values of family and friendship, social acceptance and support. Figurative images are very often "sweet," often cute, heartwarming, sometimes gushingly sentimental, or, less commonly, tension-reducing through humor, as in Figure 13. In online interviews with ops, many characterized *rainbow* as "a family."

The folklorist John Michael Vlac (1992: 19) has pointed out that "Th concept of group art implies, inde requires, that artists acquire their abilities, both manual and intellectual, at least in part from communication with others." Certainly, this is true for *rainbow* artists and players. The primary duty of ops is to teach others how create and display the art. And we have seen that some forms of the art are the focus of scheduled shows, which scores of players an even casual visitors to the channel attend. The art is a means to celebrate holidays as well as some players' birthdays. Most of all, as this article has shown in countless ways, the art is itself a form of communication: one experiences i either while displaying or viewing i primarily in real-time communication with others. The players have a strong sense of "co presence," despite the mediated nature of their interaction (Biocca 1997; Lombard and Ditton 1997; Jacobson 2002).

In recent discussions of folk art we sometimes encountered ostensibly alternative terms such a "naïve art" and "outsider art" (Zolberg and Cherbo 1997; Fine, in preparation). In fact, whereas individuals labeled naive or outsid artists typically work alone, folk artists work in a group context. "Folk art says 'We are,' but the works of [naive artists] cry 'I am'" (Crease and Mann 1983: 91, cited i Dubin 1997: 39). In this sense *rainbow* art is quintessentially folk

What of the craft aspects of *rainbow* imagery? Here too there are glaring anomalies, at first sigh As I wrote in *Cyberpl@y* (Danet 2001):

. prima facie, *the case for this*
rm of expression as craft seems
st. Craft involves the
emonstration of skill in the
anipulation of material with
ne's hands and careful eye–
and coordination. Not only did
is art lack physicality, but our
aditional notion of the
handmade" seems totally
rapplicable. Surely, a
rachine—the computer—has
ken over the work of the hand
nd therefore one may no longer
peak of craft. (Danet 2001: 253)

ny would argue, even
ementely, that *rainbow* "quilting"
ks the satisfactions of traditional
ilting. Judy Elsley beautifully
rculated some of these
tisfactions for quilters:

Quilting is quiet, slow,
editative work. The quilter
enters on the regular, rocking
rovement of the needle, feeling
he subtle ridges of cotton form
nder her fingers. She focuses
n her needle, her fingers, her
hread, her breathing, and the
letail of her quilt. Quilting is
actile, sensual, spiritual work.
Elsley 1996: 53)

Henry Lucie-Smith divided the
story of craft into three stages: the
te when all was craft; the period
rm the Renaissance to the
Industrial Revolution, when craft
bcame differentiated from fine art;
d the period since the Industrial
Rvolution, during which craft
bjects became differentiated from
Industrial products made by
machines (Lucie-Smith 1981: 11).
Malcolm McCullough (1996) has
sggested that in the digital era we

should add a new stage to the
history of craft:

In digital production, craft refers
to the condition where people
apply standard technological
means to unanticipated or
indescribable ends. Works of
computer animation, geometric
modeling, and spatial databases
get "crafted" when experts use
limited software capacities
resourcefully, imaginatively, and
in compensation for the
inadequacies of prepackaged,
hard-coded operations . . . To
craft is to care . . . to craft implies
working at a personal scale—
acting locally in reaction to
anonymous, globalized,
industrial production.
(McCullough 1996: 21–2,
emphasis added)

Careful eye–hand coordination is
important in the creation of *rainbow*
art too. Moreover, the players even
occasionally use the term
"handmade:" like some ASCII
artists, *rainbow* artists sometimes
speak of their creations as
"handmade" if "drawn" or even
edited in a word-processing
program like Notepad, rather than
using a conversion program that
automatically transforms a
conventional graphic image into a
text-based one.[27] Most forms of
handwork involve the use of some
kind of tool; ultimately it is
meaningless to ask what is truly
made by hand. What is critical is the
matter of control: "Continuous
control of process is at the heart of
tool usage and craft practice"
(McCullough 1996: 66).

In 2001 the Museum of
International Folk Art in Santa Fe,

New Mexico sponsored a pioneering
exhibition entitled "Cyber Arte:
Tradition Meets Technology." The
exhibition was described as
containing works of tangible
substance by four contemporary
Hispana/Chicana/Latina artists who
combine elements traditionally
defined as "folk" with current
computer technology. This was the
first public presentation by this
museum (or any other, as far as I
know) of digitally produced
phenomena that museum staff
members called "folk." Note,
however, that in this case
computers were used to create
tangible objects. While this
exhibition was important for setting
a precedent—recognition of the
possibility of "folk" art created with
computers—institutional
legitimation should not be a
substitute for direct evidence about
the art itself. This article has
attempted to provide such
evidence.[28]

Notes

1. This article is based on portions
   of a manuscript in progress,
   tentatively titled *Pixel*
   Patchwork: An Online Folk Art
   Community and Its Art (Danet in
   preparation). For an earlier
   report on this topic, see
   Cyberpl@y: Communicating
   Online (Danet 2001), Chapter 6,
   also available online as the
   sample chapter at the book's
   companion website, http://
   atar.mscc.huji.ac.il/~msdanet/
   cyberpl@y/. The Internet
   Explorer version also contains all
   illustrations; the Netscape
   version is text only.
2. The channel has long had its
   own website. In June 2002 a

previous website was removed, when its webmistress and channel leader, ‹patches›, left IRC. Various versions of this website, 1998–2002, can still be viewed at the Internet Archive, at http://web.archive.org/web/*/ http://www.mirc-rainbow.com/. In Fall 2002 a new website was created, though still in a rather preliminary stage, at http:// www.mirc-rainbow.net/ index.html.

3. This shareware program was developed by Khaled Mardam-Bey. See http:// www.mirc.co.uk/. He transformed a previously text-only program, that had been in existence since 1988, into a Windows-based one that could accommodate use of color, though he did not anticipate that this would lead to an art form. He merely intended color to be available to enhance verbal text.

4. There is no substitute for viewing this phenomenon in real time online. To do so, download and install mIRC for Windows from http://www.mirc.co.uk/ or linked sites. Once the program is activated, choose an Undernet server, and when logged onto it, type /join #mirc_rainbow in the main window.

5. All nicks are presented in angle brackets, just as they appear online.

6. For an overview of these varieties of text art, together with illustrations, see Danet (2001: 197–207).

7. ASCII is an acronym for American Standard Code for Information Interchange; it specified the set of ninety-five

typographic characters than c be used in plain text across a platforms online, as in e-mail An unintended consequence decision-making regarding th issue is that because the developers of these technologies were largely American, the code favors the writing system of English. On the history of ASCII art, see Danet (2001), Chapter 5. See also my discussion below abc the so-called extended ASCII characters, e.g. those unique specific languages and not usable in ordinary e-mail.

8. Images are stored in a database, created with a program called Image AXS Prc

9. See http://www.afn.org/ ~afn39695/veilleux.htm.

10. Stark's ASCII art gallery is not currently accessible, but may still be viewed at the Internet Archive http://web.archive.or web/*/http:// www.geocities.com/SoHo/ 7373/. See also Danet (2001: 228–30). Because her work is so often adapted by *rainbow* artists, many have downloade her collections for their private use, thus relieving them of dependence on the website.

11. See Glassie (1989); Paine (1990); Pellman (1984); Purdo (1996); von Gwinner (1988).

12. See, e.g. Laurel (1991); McMill (2002); Rafaeli and Sudweeks (1998); Schultz (2000).

13. "From 1840 to 1875, friendship quilts were made in staggering numbers by a broad cross section of American women" (Lipsett 1997: 19). See also Cla (1986); von Gwinner (1988: 133–9).

I am grateful to Brian Wells Galusha, who created the page at http://www.rootsweb.com/ ~nycayuga/quilt/#quilt, where I learned of this quilt, for providing the images in Figure 7 and for granting permission to reproduce them in this article. For further information, see this URL.

The URL for this webring is http://suzieque.net/ quiltingcircle.htm. Some digital quilters are creating secondary "quilts" composed of their own photographs. See http:// www.grammyj.com/ QCOFfriends.html.

The site is self-described as "devoted to pushing the limits of collaborative artwork." See http://ice.tiles.org/. On earlier computer underground art, see Danet (2001: 233–4).

Personal e-mail communication from Jon Shirin, 3 January 2003. One can see in Figure 9 where tiles were still missing, marked by the expression "coming soon."

If unexpectedly one is disconnected, images recently displayed remain visible as long as the program is open and the buffer contains them. The size of the buffer can also be increased beyond the default setting, but it is not infinite.

Source: The *Grove Dictionary of Art*, http://www.groveart.com/.

These are dictionary definitions.

Figure 4 is an unusually elaborate example of heraldic symmetry, a special case of bilateral or mirror symmetry, in *rainbow* art. Known from ancient times, in heraldic arrangements, "paired animals [are] arranged symmetrically to either side of an intervening central element" (Riegl 1992 [1893]: 41). Sometimes, pairs of human beings are displayed this way too. Typically, the head of the animal is portrayed frontally, while the body is shown in profile, as in Figure 4. My database includes perhaps a dozen examples of simpler heraldic symmetry, just one pair of animals portrayed this way.

22. The mixing of serious and playful elements is by no means unique to *rainbow* art and communication, and may be emerging as a feature of online ritual generally, including religious ritual. See Danet (in press) for a discussion of *rainbow* art and communication as a form of secular, ritualized play.

23. ASCII images seemingly "float" in undefined space, and are usually strung together one after the other in large files, stored on the web. See Danet (in preparation), Chapter 4, for a discussion of the significance of demarcation of the surrounding space in *rainbow* art.

24. For a fuller exposition of the notion of good gestalt, see Kreitler and Kreitler (1972), Chapter 4. On gestalt theory generally and processes in the perception of art, see Arnheim (1974); Gombrich (1984); Herrnstein-Smith (1968); Koffka (1935); Kohler (1929); Solso (1996), Chapter 4.

25. Members of the "in group," on the other hand, hardly need to sweep the cursor over an image to identify it. They tend to know and collect each others' work, and to recognize the style of the ASCII artist whose work has been appropriated.

26. In earlier research I had identified only five strategies. See Danet (2001: 258–69) and Figure 6.5.

27. Joan Stark noted on her ASCII art website that she "draws" her creations by hand, rather than using a conversion program. Cf. the creations of Allen Mullen, another ASCII artist, who openly used such a conversion program extensively, and consequently called them "pictures" rather than "art." See http://www.inetw.net/ ~mullen/index.html.

28. Ironically, while the website of this museum continues to offer online versions of past shows of physical objects, there was never an online version of the "Cyber Arte" exhibit, except for a temporary general introduction to it, which is no longer available. See http://www.moifa.org/.

References

Arnheim, Rudolf. 1974. *Art and Visual Perception: A Psychology of the Creative Eye*. Berkeley CA: University of California Press.

Batchelor, David. 2001. *Chromophobia*. London: Reaktion.

Ben-Amos, Dan. 1971. "Toward a Definition of Folklore in Context." *Journal of American Folklore* 84: 3–15.

Biocca, Frank. 1997. "The Cyborg's Dilemma: Progressive Embodiment in Virtual Environments." *Journal of Computer-Mediated Communication*

3. http://www.ascusc.org/jcmc/vol3/issue2.

Clark, Ricky. 1986. "Mid Nineteenth Century Album and Friendship Quilts 1860–1920." In Jeannette Lasansky (ed.), *Pieced by Mother: Symposium Papers*, pp. 77–86. Lewisburg, PA: University of Pennsylvania Press.

Crease, Robert and Charles Mann. 1983. "Backyard Creators of Art That Says: 'I Did It, I'm Here'." *Smithsonian Magazine* 14, 82–91.

Danet, Brenda. 2001. *Cyberpl@y: Communicating Online*. Oxford: Berg Publishers. Companion website: http://atar.mscc.huji.ac.il/~msdanet/cyberpl@y/ (best viewed in Internet Explorer).

——. In press. "Play, Art and Ritual on IRC (Internet Relay Chat)." In Eric W. Rothenbuhler and Mihai Coman (eds), *Media Anthropology*.

——. In preparation. *Pixel Patchwork: An Online Folk Art Community and Its Art*.

Dewhurst, C. Kurt, Betty McDowell and Marsha Macdowell. 1979. *Artists in Aprons: Folk Art by American Women*. New York: E. P. Dutton with the Museum of American Folk Art.

Dubin, Steven C. 1997. "The Centrality of Marginality: Naive Artists and Savvy Supporters." In Vera L. Zolberg and Joni Maya Cherbo (eds), *Outsider Art: Contesting Boundaries in Contemporary Culture*, pp. 37–52. Cambridge: Cambridge University Press.

Elsley, Judy. 1996. *Quilts as Text(iles): The Semiotics of Quilting*. New York: Peter Lang.

Fine, Gary Alan. In press. *Everyday Genius: Self-Taught Art and the Politics of Authenticity*. Chicago: University of Chicago Press.

Glassie, Henry. 1989. *The Spirit of Folk Art*. New York and Santa Fe NM: Harry N. Abrams and Museum of New Mexico.

Gombrich, Ernst. 1984. *The Sense of Order: A Study in the Psychology of Decorative Art*. London: Phaidon.

Herrnstein-Smith, Barbara. 1968. *Poetic Closure: A Study of How Poems End*. Chicago IL: University of Chicago Press.

——. 1978. *On the Margins of Discourse: The Relation of Literature to Language*. Chicago IL: University of Chicago Press.

Hibi, Sadao. 2000. *The Colors of Japan*. Tokyo: Kodansha International and Kodansha, America.

Jacobson, David. 2002. "On Theorizing Presence." *Journal of Virtual Environments* 6. www.brandeis.edu/pubs/jove/HTML/v6/presence.HTML.

Koffka, K. 1935. *Principles of Gestalt Psychology*. New York: Harcourt Brace.

Kohler, W. 1929. *Gestalt Psychology*. New York: Liveright.

Kreitler, Hans and Shulamith Kreitler. 1972. *Psychology of the Arts*. Durham NC: University of North Carolina Press.

Laurel, Brenda. 1991. *Computers as Theatre*. Reading MA: Addison-Wesley.

Lichtenstein, Jacqueline. 1993. *The Eloquence of Color: Rhetoric and Painting in the French Classical Age*.

rkeley, CA: University of California ess.

sett, Linda Otto. 1997. *Remember e: Women and Their Friendship uilts*. Lincolnwood IL: Quilt Digest ess.

mbard, Matthew and Teresa tton. 1997. "At the Heart of It All: e Concept of Telepresence." *urnal of Computer-Mediated mmunication* 3. http:// ww.ascusc.org/jcmc/vol3/issue2/ mbard.html.

cie-Smith, Edward. 1981. *The ory of Craft: The Craftsman's Role Society*. Oxford: Phaidon.

cCullough, Malcolm. 1996. *stracting Craft*. Cambridge MA: IT Press.

cMillan, Sally J. 2002. "A Four-part odel of Cyber-interactivity." *New edia & Society* 4: 271–91.

ine, Sheila. 1990. *Embroidered xtiles: Traditional Patterns from ve Continents*. London: Thames & udson.

rola, Rene. 1996. *Optical Art: eory and Practice*. New York: over, originally published by einhold, New York, 1969.

ellman, Rachel and Kenneth ellman. 1984. *The World of Amish uilts*. Intercourse PA: Good Books.

illips, Peter and Gillian Bunce. 93. *Repeat Patterns: A Manual for*

Designers, Artists and Architects. London: Thames & Hudson.

Pocius, Gerald L. 1979. "Hooked Rugs in Newfoundland: The Representation of Social Structure in Design." *Journal of American Folklore* 92: 273–84.

Purdon, Nicholas. 1996. *Carpet and Textile Patterns*. London: Lawrence King.

Rafaeli, Sheizaf and Fay Sudweeks. 1998. "Interactivity on the Nets." In Fay Sudweeks, Margaret McLaughlin and Sheizaf Rafaeli (eds), *Network and Netplay: Virtual Groups on the Internet*, pp. 173–90. Menlo Park, CA and Cambridge MA: AAAI Press and MIT Press.

Riegl, Alois. 1992 [1893]. *Problems of Style: Foundations for a History of Ornament*. Princeton NJ: Princeton University Press.

Riley, Charles A., II. 1995. *Color Codes: Modern Theories of Color in Philosophy, Painting and Architecture, Literature, Music and Psychology*. Hanover NH: University of New England Press.

Schultz, Tanjev. 2000. "Mass Media and the Concept of Interactivity: an Exploratory Study of Online Forums and Reader Email." *Media, Culture and Society* 22: 205–21.

Solso, Robert L. 1996. *Cognition and the Visual Arts*. Cambridge MA: MIT Press.

Trilling, James. 2001. *The Language of Ornament*. London: Thames & Hudson.

Turner, Victor. 1969. *The Ritual Process: Structure and Anti-Structure*. Chicago, IL: Aldine.

——. 1974. *Dramas, Fields, and Metaphors: Symbolic Action in Human Society*. Ithaca NY: Cornell University Press.

Varichon, Anne. 2000. *Couleurs: pigments et teintures dans les mains des peuples*. Paris: Seuil.

Vlach, John Michael. 1992. "Properly Speaking: The Need for Plain Talk About Folk Art." In John Michael Vlach and Simon J. Bronner (eds), *Folk Art and Art Worlds*, pp. 13–26. Logan, UT: Utah State University Press.

von Gwinner, Schnuppe. 1988. *The History of the Patchwork Quilt: Origins, Traditions and Symbols of a Textile Art*. West Chester PA: Schiffer.

Weyl, Hermann. 1952. *Symmetry*. Princeton NJ: Princeton University Press.

Yabsley, Suzanne. 1984. *Texas Quilts, Texas Women*. College Station TX: Texas A & M University.

Zolberg, Vera L. and Joni Maya Cherbo (eds). 1997. *Outsider Art: Contesting Boundaries in Contemporary Culture*. Cambridge: Cambridge University Press.

India Inside Out: Critical Perspectives on the Work of Mrinalini Mukherjee

Abstract

This essay examines the critical responses, both in the UK and India, to the work of Mrinalini Mukherjee, a well known artist whose woven and majestic forms cross over between sculpture and textiles. The essay traces the ways in which Mukherjee's art was increasingly associated with religious questions during the 1990s, and situates this tendency in the context of the rise of religious fundamentalism within India. The energetic trade of "orientalizing" perspectives on Mukherjee's art between the UK and India has largely diverted attention from Mukherjee's core artistic concerns and the processes, histories and influences that have inspired her. Amongst her major influences are the writings and philosophy of Rabindranath Tagore, the teachings of K. G. Subramanyan and the sculptures of Ram Kinkar Baij. This analysis of art criticism around Mukherjee's art raises the problems facing contemporary artists in post-colonialist contexts.

CTORIA LYNN

ɔria Lynn is Director, Creative Development,
tralian Centre for the Moving Image. She
anized the 1993 exhibition *India Songs: Multiple*
ams *in Contemporary Indian Art* in Sydney, and the
an section of the 1996 *Asia Pacific Triennale*,
sbane.

Textile, Volume 1, Issue 2, pp. 144–156
Reprints available directly from the Publishers.

India Inside Out: Critical Perspectives on the Work of Mrinalini Mukherjee

Knotting jute into organic forms that resemble large, succulent flowers and fecund figures, Mrinalini Mukherjee created a body of monumental works during the 1990s that have an enduring, at times uncanny, quality. Mukherjee is a leading Indian sculptor whose work has always challenged the accepted ways in which art, craft, and modernism are discussed and appreciated both within and outside of India. She worked with hand-dyed jute and rope from her student days until the late 1990s (more recently she embraced ceramics to create equally compelling abstract constellations of fired forms). For decades, Mukherjee's work has faced a critical resistance within India. This was largely due to the fact that her large woven sculptures participate in the discourses on both modernism and craft. In India, as in the United Kingdom, there has been a tendency to discount the work of artists using textiles as belonging to a set of traditions outside of modernism. This is despite the fact that the early-nineteenth-century art schools in India were actually established with the intention of preserving the crafts of India, albeit for industrial purposes. However, as the schools developed into the late-nineteenth century, a formalized and academic education in the art of drawing, painting, and sculpture gradually dominated and an enthusiasm for the "high arts" replaced the intere in the arts of the artisan classes. A least two art schools attempted to redress this in the latter half of the twentieth century and Mukherjee' own work has been formulated through exposure to both of these schools. Nevertheless, the prejudices of the academic art school model continue to linger within India.

During the 1990s, Mukherjee's art came to be apprehended not s much in terms of its relationship t craft, or to folk traditions, but rathe in terms of its supposed religious references. This was the case in both India and the United Kingdo The alignment of her work with ov religious content paralleled, withi India, the rise to power of the Hind BJP party, along with an increase i religious and social discord. In the face of the increasing connection between religion and conservative politics, many artists voiced what came to be called a "secular" poir of view. In the United Kingdom, Mukherjee was being recognized and applauded for the complete "otherness" of her works, while in India her interest in folk deities wa regarded as a kind of naive and apolitical spiritualism. The followi discussion of the critical framewo for Mukerhjee's art, both inside a outside India, reveals an energetic trade in these two perspectives which ultimately participate in a form of "orientalizing" of the work

a discussion that has largely
erted attention from Mukherjee's
e artistic concerns and the
cesses, histories, and influences
t have inspired her. Edward Said
commented: "what matters a
at deal more than the stable
ntity kept current in official
course is the contestatory force
an interpretative method whose
terial is the disparate, but
ertwined and interdependent,
d above all overlapping streams
istorical experience" (Said 1993:
).

Born in Bombay (Mumbai) in
9, Mrinalini Mukherjee comes
m a rather unconventional artist
ily and has, throughout her
eer, filtered a range of influences
'streams of historical
erience." Her father,
nodebihari, was a well-known
ralist and painter; her mother,
la, a painter and sculptor. While
kherjee was growing up, her
her taught at a major art school
rth of Calcutta, Santiniketan. The
os of this school was based on
writings of Rabindranath Tagore
61–1941), its founder, and the
losophies of Tagore have
ormed Mukherjee's work.
rinalini was named after Tagore's
e.) Tagore believed that art
ould have a communion with
ture. He commented that "for our
rfection we have to be vitally
vage and mentally civilized; we
ould have the gift to be natural
h nature and human with man"
onson 1986: 30). In his essay on
e Meaning of Art, he wrote that
his creative activities man
kes nature instinct with his own
and love" (Tagore 1921: 22).
ile Tagore did not embrace any
ecific religion, he clearly did

believe that the creativity of
individuals has the capacity to be
divine. Tagore was adamantly
opposed to nationalism of any kind
and, for this reason, has been called
a modernist.

At the age of sixteen Mrinalini
Mukherjee attended art school in
Baroda, a city that lies between New
Delhi and Mumbai. Many of the
senior teachers at Baroda had
studied at Santiniketan. From 1971,
aged 22, she began to experiment
with fiber—jute and hemp—and
made large-scale wall hangings and
suspended forms. Her principal
teacher was K. G. Subramanyan
(also one of her father's students), a
proponent of the notion that art
needs to have an integral
connection with craft. The Baroda
art school included lessons in mural
painting, mosaics, ceramics, and
weaving along with sculpture,
painting, and print-making. There
was an enthusiasm not only for
modernism in painting and
sculpture, but also the rural and
tribal visual cultures of India. Nilima
Sheikh, an artist and former lecturer
at Baroda, comments, "visiting folk
melas and tribal haats [festivals],
travelling into rural and forest
interiors, was as much a part of the
motivated student's curriculum as
the more organized study tours" (N.
Sheikh 1997: 116).

A third influence on the art of
Mrinalini Mukherjee is the large-
scale bronze- and cement-cast
figurative sculptures of Ram Kinkar
Baij, one of India's foremost
modernist sculptors who also
taught at Santiniketan. The
physicality, scale, and
monumentality of Ram Kinkar Baij's
work has been inspirational for
Mrinalini Mukherjee. (Her mother

was also Baij's student at
Santiniketan.) Despite her
admiration for his work, Mukherjee
relates the story that Ram Kinkar
Baij did not appreciate her own
forays into rope. At Santiniketan,
sculpture was generally taught with
reference to a notion of
international modernism, in
particular, the work of Constantine
Brancusi and Henry Moore. Ram
Kinkar Baij's own work involved a
form of intensely emotional
figurative expressionism common
also to some modernist Indian
painting.

Mrinalini Mukherjee was invited
by the Museum of Modern Art in
Oxford to have a one-person
exhibition which was held from 17
April to 19 June 1994 (Elliot 1994).
The show included a group of free-
standing woven sculptures. Woman
on Peacock, 1991, a central piece in
the exhibition, is a large imposing
figurative form woven from a
tapestry of dark purple, green, gold,
and blue knots (Figure 1). Here is the
connection between a human and
an animal realm, but also between a
female and male sexuality. This
imperceptible marriage of opposites
through the weave of Mukherjee's
hand is a kind of riposte to Ram
Kinkar Baij's monumental male
figures. Another exceptional work
from this series is Pushp (The
flower), 1993, a spherical, red and
golden form with folds within folds
of knotted layers (Figure 2). It is at
once sensual and formidable. It has
a presence beyond its size. Not only
does Pushp refer to the flower; its
medium is in direct communion with
nature and with the folk traditions
that actively use hemp and jute in a
daily context (for instance, it is used
for making the bags that hold

onions). And yet *Pushp* recalls the abstract forms of international modernist sculpture. The artist constructs a rudimentary metal frame and then begins to weave from the top downwards. This process requires that the weaving cannot be reversed and the sculptures tend to take on their own life force as the artist creates the cascading and protruding layers of rope. In some instances, these soft sculptures like to sit in their own way against the wall, or on the floor, taking a slightly different configuration on each occasion. In many respects, they possess their own character, and they work best visually in groups where there is an active dialogue and where there is a relational, architectural framework for this dialogue. It is no accident that Mukherjee is fascinated by archaeological sites and ruined buildings in India and elsewhere.

Two of the catalog essays for the Oxford Museum of Modern Art exhibition are short texts, almost testimonials, by fellow Indian artists and writers Gulammohammed Sheikh and J. Swaminathan. Both artists aim to elevate the meanings inherent in the works to the highest levels. Given that Mukherjee's struggle prior to this had been to gain acceptance in India as a sculptor rather than a craftsperson, it is not surprising that these texts are written in a manner that seeks to prove her credentials as an artist dealing with time-honored principles.

Gulammohammed Sheikh comments that craft—"as domestic girls plaiting their hair, or women knotting string cots"—is "turned into a magic formula by the intervening artifice of the artist's

hands" (G. Sheikh 1994: 5). He th goes on to suggest that these wo are more than the sum of their parts, more than the knotting of fiber:

Swelling outwards and breathin from its multiple pores, the image in its pachyderm monumentality—suffused with abundant sensuality—extends it span beyond its physical reach. If the fibrous deities stand in each other's company, the surrounding spaces begin to become animated with enigmat presence. Her installations often evoke sensations of the spaces arboreal shrines. The viewer, lik the spirits, is enticed into the orbit of the image's magnetic field, to invest all his emotions, memories and associations in order to view the world through these stringed volumes.

He compares these works to three ancient Indian forms of sculpture: the *Yakshi*, the female counterpar of a forest deity as seen in the sensual Mathura sculptures; the *Naga*, a serpent deity with a hood human head found in the shrines situated on village outskirts; and *Bhuta*, large wooden figures of cu spirits from the coast of Karnatak Sheikh argues that Mrinalini Mukherjee's use of fiber "radicalizes the meaning of magic because she has not used the ancient stone or wood. Fibre, he says, "makes a fresh aesthetic assertion as a metaphor of resistance to conventional norms. None of Sheikh's references to ancient sculptural forms in India refer to one specific religion, and is careful to propose an innovativ roach in Mrinalini Mukherjee's nsformation of sculptural ditions into new aesthetic forms. J. Swaminathan's short text also nts to the uniqueness of kherjee's choice of vegetable er, rather than stone, wood, clay, ster or metal. He emphasizes the undity, eroticism, "the miasmic of a tropical fruit" (Swaminathan 04: 6). Then he also conjures ecifically Indian references by ggesting that the work converses h the image of the mother ddess:

Erotic in the purest sense, Mukherjee's work aspires to the sublime: in partaking of stone and water, mineral and air, the pulsating heat of the fibre of life in her sculpture aspires to immortality through proliferation as Prakati, and to a self-contained equilibrium as Chinnamasta. (Prakati and Chinnamasta are two aspects of the Mother Goddess: one as Nature in its endless variety and one as self-sustaining power, holding her severed head in one

hand and drinking her own blood.)

There are two other texts in the Oxford Museum of Art catalog. One is the introduction by Director David Elliot and the other is an interview by Chrissie Iles. Each of them has structured their text as a response not only to the works, but also the texts by Sheikh and Swaminathan, resulting in a set of conclusions about the work that tends to orientalize it. Elliot writes, "Time and process are . . . imprinted in

gure 1
inalini Mukherjee, *Woman on Peacock*, 91. Courtesy the artist. Photograph: inash Pasricha.

numinous and natural presence which emanates from each work. This form of non-specific aesthetic animism, . . . which Tagore himself may have recognized, positions Mukherjee's work within its Indian context," a broad statement which suggests that the "Indian context" is one in which "animism" is central (Elliot 1994: 4). There is no reference to specific histories of modernism in India, or the work's formal relationship to modernist sculptu, or ancient architecture.

As analyzed in an article in *Th, Text* in 1994 by Tania Guha, the interview with Mrinalini Mukherje in the Oxford Museum catalog by Chrissie Iles follows a similar line inquiry (Guha 1994: 165–8). After Mrinalini Mukherjee suggests tha her work develops along intuitive, formal lines, a "tier-by-tier growth "a process of growth," Iles asks if

Figure 2
Mrinalini Mukherjee, *Pushp*, 1993.
Courtesy the artist. Photograph: Auinash
Pasricha.

gests a "pre-technological way of knowing the world" (Iles 1994: 15). Mukherjee says she simply es the material—the look and feel of it, and its inexpensive nature. She comments:

India we do not talk about a pre-technological way of knowing the world" since, as well s the urban artists, there are undreds of artists and raftsmen working in rural areas, sing the natural materials vailable to them. In India their rts have always existed longside each other, at different levels of sophistication. India as an enormous wealth of craft, nd I believe in an integrated pproach to art and craft, so I njoy working with the "linguistics" developed by the ractice of craft. It is through my elationship to my material that I vould like to reach out and align myself with the values which xist within the ambit of ontemporary sculpture.

Iles then goes on to ask whether e colors relate to "its ceremonial d ritual function in Indian life." ukherjee says her color is rsonal and "has no relationship traditional iconography." Iles en asks if the works "house irits." Mukherjee says she loved e garden towns in which she grew and her work has gradually ought in the human, or uperhuman." While referring to e works as "anthropomorphic ities" she says her "mythology is conventionalized and personal." ukherjee is clearly trying to ggest a position and practice that s between the influences of her

youth: Indian modernism, Tagore's philosophy, Subramanyan's embracement of craft, a love of nature, and the belief that sculpture can inspire awe.

Iles then asks "what does the sacred mean to you?" Mukherjee responds:

My idea of the sacred is not rooted in any specific culture. To me it is a feeling that I may get in a church, mosque, temple or forest. The countryside is filled with places where divinity dwells. I do not enjoy going to active temples or places of worship; I prefer archaeological sites. It is often a sense of space, scale or presence that gives me a sacred feeling, and this could occur anywhere in the world. My inspiration and visual stimuli come from all over the world, from museum objects and artifacts and, more immediately, from my environment . . . My work is not . . . the iconic representation of any particular religious belief.

Iles again: "What role do gods and goddesses play in your work, and is reincarnation significant?" Mukherjee says there's no relationship with specific gods and goddesses. Iles then asks if the work Pushp (The Flower) recalls Hindu imagery. Mukherjee says Pushp started with the image of a magnolia flower fallen from a tree. Iles then makes a comparison between the sensuality in Mukherjee's work and sexual power in images in India of the Goddess Kali. Mukherjee explains that "traditional Indian sculpture often displays male and female sexuality

explicitly, and since it is something I have been used to seeing since childhood, I have no inhibitions in representing it in my work." Finally Mukherjee says:

I do not think India rejects modernism. My own questioning of modernism is contained within the process of my work, which does not rule out modernist options but uses them for my own needs, in my particular context. I do this neither out of ideological preference, nor in opposition to Western modernist values in art.

Iles's questions are framed in terms of naturalism, animism, ritual and specific religious associations. Perhaps Iles was simply asking the questions that she thought audiences might ask, but it seems that she is intent on proving that Mukherjee's art does not simply amount to a derivative interpretation of European modernism. Every effort is made to link her work with primitive and timeless origins. Guha comments:

Iles' critical methodology is symptomatic of a romantic postmodernism that is happy to embrace other cultures so long as they can be seen to embody a diametrically opposed Other to European modernism. In order to qualify for a position in this "benevolently" pluralistic cultural arena, Mukherjee must be seen to address a different set of issues and concerns to western artists, for instance in their sense of spiritual dissolution and urban alienation *in the wake of industrialization or their shift away from naturalistic representation. (Guha 1994: 168)*

In this context, it is interesting to reconsider the degree to which the texts by the Indian artists Sheikh and Swaminathan also partake, perhaps unwittingly, of this discourse. In many respects, they seek to elevate her work from the realm of craft to the realm of high art and do so by loose associations with arboreal deities and the fecundity and sexuality that pervades a range of Indian sculptural traditions. They do not, however, suggest that Mukherjee herself subscribes to a particular set of religious beliefs; that she identifies with certain gods or goddesses or that she believes in reincarnation.

The exhibition traveled from Oxford to Yorkshire Sculpture Park and the Royal Festival Galleries in London. It received a modest amount of attention in the British press. Most of the journalistic responses expanded upon the catalog essays and Chrissie Iles's interview. Timothy Hyman, who worked in India for many years and is the author of a book on the eminent Indian artist Bhupen Khakhar, wrote in the *London Magazine* that along with Anish Kapoor and Shirazeh Houshiary, Mukherjee's work "enters our culture as a new orientalism" (Hyman 1994: 120). A comment like this provokes problematical questions about the desire to appear oriental in contemporary culture.

In the magazine *Women's Art*, Deanna Petherbridge "gazes at sculpture from outerspace," as the by-line has it (Petherbridge 1994: 26). She recognizes that "at the moment that [Mukherjee's] work i presented outside India, she is entrapped into the very discourse of ethnicity and religious identity with which she feels the least affiliation." Mukherjee, Petherbridge comments, takes inspiration from folk myths and artifacts and does so without naivety, but also without engaging with "the discourses of power, psychoanalysis, anthropology or feminism." In this way, Petherbridge locates Mukherjee's works as "allusive," "but do not ti her into . . . traditionalism," simila she suggests, to the Pegasus imagery of Christopher LeBrun.

Prior to the Oxford Museum of Art exhibition returning to India, some promotional texts appeared the local Indian news press. As the writers had not seen the exhibition these pieces mostly used the catalog as a resource. In an article titled "Contemporary Indian Sculpture," August/September 1995, the *Indialink International Magazine* comments, "the rough, fibrous material and the repetitive hand-made construction suggest a pre-technological understanding c the world, in which metamorphosi and the sacred are strongly preser Her volumes embrace the inseparable unity of nature and culture which lies at the heart of Indian aesthetics and philosophy. Seemingly unaware of the orientalism at play in these comments, the writer has offered r independent interpretation of the terms used in the catalog, nor has he acknowledged Mukherjee's own responses to Iles's assumptions about Indian culture.

In an article titled "Creative
re" published in *Expression*, the
ia Express Sunday Magazine, 27
bruary 1994, Prema Viswanathan
s a more balanced view of the
ulptures by pointing to what she
ms a "dialectic" in the work:
ere is the languor of a hothouse
ant, the voluptuousness of an
sara [a heavenly female form
and on early Buddhist shrines],
e reassurance of a mother-figure,
d the awesomeness of a deity.
t at another level, there is also an
ement of abstraction, as each
ure transforms itself into a free
wing form." Further, "it is this
alectic in Mrinalini's forms that
lps them transcend the barrier
tween art and craft, a divide that
e feels needs to be bridged."
swanathan's point of view has
en informed by her interview with
ukherjee, whom she quotes as
king, "Did our ancient sculptors
 muralists ever pause to think
ether they were craftsmen or
tists?" Viswanathan concludes by
sorting to a form of feminine
sentialism, commenting that the
rms "appear almost to have come
at of her womb, the unborn
aildren of her past and her future."
The exhibition returned to India
ad was displayed at the British
buncil Art Gallery in New Delhi
om 26 September to 14 October
·95. In an article titled "Weaving in
me" in *The Pioneer* newspaper, 19
ctober 1995, M. L. Johny and
rinal Kulkari present a more
sightful analysis of the critical
erception of Mukherjee's work.
ter claiming "Mrinalini's works
voke a remoteness of traditional
tforms and archaeological sites,"
ey suggest that her work has been
aracterized as "anti-modernist by

western critics . . . [who] try to make
her an artist of exotica and erotica.
The post-modernist way of looking
at them questions her presence as
an author, and with a concealed
despise place her in [*sic*] an anti-
modernist pedestal." In relation to
this post-modernist perspective (for
which they give no examples) they
argue that "the writing out of
authorial presence" is problematic
in India. Mukherjee's work is
modernist, they claim, but she also
questions modernism.

In a sharply critical article titled
"Oriental Reflection in Sculpture" in
another newspaper, *The Statesman*,
2 October 1995, M. Ramachandran
also assesses the responses to
Mukherjee's work at an
international level. "What G. M.
Sheikh discerns as 'the iconic
images of numinous import,' and
Swaminathan senses as 'the secret
and sacred primordial powers in the
iconic splendor,' are nothing but the
same 'Indianess' the Westerners
seek from Indian artists."
Ramachandran then depicts the
artist as a kind of evil seductress by
saying, "one has to beware of the
seductive charm and inviting
eroticism of Mrinalini Mukherjee's
Yakshis, their grove and flowers."
Equating her work with Tantric
painting in India during the 1960s,
the Hindu philosophy that
"celebrates sexuality," the critic
classifies her work in the realm of a
"market-oriented indigenism." That
is, he blames the work for the
orientalist discourse within which it
is trapped. His criticism does not
come close to understanding the
forces at work in Mrinalini
Mukherjee's woven sculpture. This
was also obvious to Mukherjee
herself, who saw the writing by two

dear artist-friends caught in a cycle
of interpretation that returned her
work to Indian audiences in an
orientalist cloak. While the media
and critical attention was no doubt
welcomed by Mukherjee, she
experienced acute frustration with
how the work was being appraised.

A further dimension to the ways
in which Mukherjee's work was, on
the one hand, acclaimed for its
exoticism in the West, and on the
other, criticized for its supposed
Hindu associations within India, is
the growth of religious
fundamentalism in India during the
1990s. In this context, Mrinalini
Mukherjee treads a fine and
complex line. There is indeed a
correspondence between the
increasing sensitivity amongst
India's creative communities to
religious fundamentalism in India,
and the criticism of Mukherjee's
work for its religious associations
which, for many, rendered it non-
contemporary and located it outside
of the history of modernism. And yet
these references framed the work's
acceptance in the United Kingdom.
In India artists, writers, film-makers,
and the like tend to position
themselves and their work in the
realm of what is termed
"secularism." That is, they eschew
religious associations—living,
practicing religious rituals or belief
systems—for these modes are taken
in the public imagination to be an
endorsement of fundamentalism,
which is, at its core, racist and
conservative. In 1992–93, just prior
to Mukherjee's exhibition in Oxford,
riots spread across India in
response to the destruction of a
Muslim temple in Ayodhya in 1990.
The violent conflicts between
Muslims and Hindus in India

continues today. While a sensitivity to socio-political issues is by no means new in modern Indian art, this rise of religious discord sharpened artists' attitudes: the violence, fear, and fierce destruction of the riots in 1992–93 is often cited within India as a catalyst for change in the work of contemporary artists. Some artists have chosen to explore the relationship between spiritual myths and violence. Others have avoided any hint of specific religious references in their work. Allusions to political threat have emerged in the art works of others. Mukherjee chose to pursue her life's work, unchallenged by contemporary events.

In addition, during the 1990s, many artists, musicians, writers, actors, and film-makers were actively involved in an organization called SAHMAT, the Sadfar Hashmi Memorial Trust, established to promote the importance of peace and advocate the values of secularism and cultural pluralism. Exhibitions, performances, and concerts are held across India on a regular basis in order to raise awareness of such values. One of the more disturbing incidents during the riot period of 1992–93 involved the seizure and destruction of a group of paintings by Indian artist M. F. Husain. Husain's house was burned. The paintings, which depicted Hindu goddesses in erotic poses, were actually painted at least ten years prior to the incident. Previously considered rather humorous and apolitical, the paintings became a political symbol in artists' struggles against religious persecution.

Perhaps in order to introduce a fresh perspective, Mukherjee invited the art critic and lecturer Deepak Ananth (based in France) write on her work for the British Council Art Gallery exhibition catalog (Ananth 1995). Tellingly, h references range from Deleuze's writings on the fold, to Anand Coomaraswamy. While situating t artist within the history of Subramanyan's teachings on the conflation of art and craft, he also points to Western artists who in th late 1960s manifested an interest the "poetics of a vernacular mode He cites French artists' interest in bricolage, the Arte Povera artists' "aesthetic of impoverishment," at Eva Hesse's post-minimalist rope work (Mukherjee did not learn of Hesse's work until the 1980s). He suggests that in their use of the "vernacular" modes is an "inadvertent eroticism" and make the very important point that in societies where the vernacular has not been vanquished, such as Ind this eroticism has little currency. (Mukherjee commented to Iles, eroticism in sculpture is a daily, almost colloquial, sight in India.) E using the rope, the vernacular of t villagers, and creating sculpture, Mukherjee's work "bespeaks an awareness of the options available for artists in a post-colonial situation." Ananth argues that Richard Long's walks in nature are response to the eclipse of nature, while Mukherjee's forms speak of an easy access to nature. Ananth sees her work as a metaphor for growth itself.

Ananth's is a refreshing text which reveals Mukherjee as both questioning and fusing the opposing terms of art/craft, masculine/feminine, "high" and "low," inside and outside, literally ough her own method of otting. The knot, he says, is a etonym of patience, repetition, station, marking time and it is a k. "A metaphorics of ncatenation might also be the ost appropriate way to describe e sensuous organic wholeness of ukherjee's sculpture." His ethodology is to go to the detail of e working process and draw in etaphoric and metonymic sociations. His approach is to mpare Mukherjee's work with estern counterparts. His eference is to think laterally about e work's inherent meanings rather an historically. Ananth's approach most useful for its metaphorical int of view that twists and turns ough French and Indian ilosophy in the same manner that ukherjee's own work folds in on elf. As such, it cuts through the scussions about art and craft, and e religious clichés that have veloped Mukherjee's art. While it kes reference to the streams of luences and histories that have ormed Mukherjee's art, however, e text tends to remain in the realm the metaphorical, which is also limitation.

One of the primary streams of luence on Mukherjee is Indian odernism. The pursuit of odernism in India is in part edicated on the desire to be seen a nation that independently oves in time (against the logic of entalism which does not allow for e colonized nation to be seen as rt of the process of history). dian modernism has an dependent trajectory that differs m the modernisms of Europe, the ited States or Australia. It has d a strong figurative, narrative,

and realist impulse which unsettles our understanding of modernism. As John Clark has written, "in relation to the discourse of modernism, it is a modern, non-Euroamerican art which subverts clarity of interpretation. The inability of a Euroamerican rhetoric to find a modern art in Asia intelligible is the very sign that its subversion will open us to the discourse of modernity itself" (Clark 1993: 16–17). Mukherjee's interest in the vernacular, and the transformation of the simple gesture of the knotting of an everyday material into a superhuman form can be seen as part of an Indian modernism (in the wake of the art schools lead by the likes of Tagore, Subramanyan, and Ram Kinkar Baij), while at the same time a rejection of the art for art's sake endpoint of international manifestations. She takes from European modernism only what is formally, and personally, relevant.

Indian theorist Geeta Kapur has commented, "the paradigm for debating cultural issues in India is not internationalism. Modernism, seen as culminating in an international style and turning on a logic of 'art for art's sake,' has not been crucial to India. Moreover, we have a modernism without an avant-garde" (Kapur 2000: 287–8). Proponents of a contemporary art in India resist any association with the folk and tribal traditions (and by implication the use of craft), for they see such associations as being open to the tendency towards nostalgia, and as the vehicle for halting forms in time. But they also resist the total adoption of the Western universalizing system of the contemporary. It has been argued by Geeta Kapur that the

resistance of the contemporary artists of India to the wholesale appropriation of the historical avant-garde, is an implied criticism of European and American modernism. Gulammohammed Sheikh has also said, "the avant-garde is also a sort of cannibalism, of devouring, reducing and taking over, making art an instrument of power. This is what many of us reacted against, and asked—as I still ask—whether there is an alternative" (Sundaram 1991: 39–40). Indeed, India is such an eclectic culture, that it is difficult for artists to embrace all that is new—the spirit of the avant-garde—and completely reject what has gone before.

Mukherjee's use of fiber, and her enthusiasm for sculptural forms from folk and ancient traditions, is best seen in this context of Indian modernism, and its resistance to the avant-garde. Just as she takes what is personally relevant from this history, so too she edits and transforms images from parallel cultural traditions in India. The work does not participate in the religious narratives of fundamentalism, nor is it a wholehearted embrace of "indigenism." As an heir to Tagore, Subramanyan, and Ram Kinkar Baij, Mukherjee found through the use of the knot, a late-twentieth century vocabulary that in fact fused, conflated, and indeed frustrated the notion that modernism, craft, and a fascination with ancient sculptural and architectural forms are mutually exclusive—as Said proposes, Mukherjee's approach brings a diversity of histories into an overlapping, intertwined visual and contemporary experience. The works of the 1990s are like beings, perhaps even self-portraits of a kind, that are so imposing, and replete with life, that they insist, almost theatrically, on their place in a post-colonial and contemporary present.

References

Ananth, Deepak. 1995. "Mrinalini Mukherjee." *Mrinalini Mukherjee, Sculpture*. New Delhi: British Council Art Gallery.

Aronson, Alex. 1986. "Tagore's Educational Ideas." *Rabrindranath Tagore A Celebration of his Life and Work*. Oxford: Museum of Modern Art.

Clark, John (ed.). 1993. "Open and Closed Discourses of Modernity in Asian Art." In *Modernity in Asian Art*. East Asian Studies no. 7, Wild Peony. Sydney: University of Sydney.

Elliot, David (ed.). 1994. *Mrinalini Mukherjee, Sculpture*. Oxford: Museum of Modern Art.

Guha, Tania. 1994. "Mrinalini Mukherjee, Labyrinths of the Mind." *Third Text* 28/29 (Autumn/Winter).

Hyman, Timothy. 1994. "Mrinalini Mukherjee at Oxford." *London Magazine* (August/September).

Iles, Chrissie. 1994. "An Interview with Mrinalini Mukherjee." *Mrinalini Mukherjee, Sculpture*. Oxford: Museum of Modern Art.

Kapur, Geeta. 2000. *When Was Modernism, Essays on Contemporary Cultural Practice in India*. New Delhi: Tulika.

Petherbridge, Deanna. 1994. "Mukherjee's Modernism." *Women's Art* (September/October).

Said, Edward W. 1993. *Culture and Imperialism*. New York: Knopf.

Sheikh, Gulammohammed. 1994. "Forms of Resilience." *Mrinalini Mukherjee, Sculpture*. Oxford: Museum of Modern Art.

Sheikh, Nilima. 1997. "A Post-Independence Initiative in Art." In Gulammohammed Sheikh (ed.) *Contemporary Art in Baroda*. New Delhi: Tulika.

Sundaram, Vivan. 1991. "A Tradition of the Modern." *Journal of Arts and Ideas* no. 20–21 (March), New Delhi.

Swaminathan, J. 1994. "Pregnant with the Sap of Fecundity: Mrinalini Mukherjee's Sculpture." *Mrinalini Mukherjee, Sculpture*. Oxford: Museum of Modern Art.

Tagore, Rabrindranath. [1921] 1983. *The Meaning of Art*. New Delhi: Lalit Kala Akademi.

The Warp of My Life

I am tied
To the warp
Of my life.
Some call it
Karma
Some call it
Genes
Some
By other names.

I do not
Fight it.
I do not
Unravel it.
I dye the weft
With my dreams,
I pluck on the
Multiple chords
Of my warp
And weave
My dreams.
My aspirations
My inner thoughts

Till it resounds
As a Raga
Of all longing
And I,
The warp
The weft
My dreams.
All merge into
The eternal ocean.
Of our Universe.
That which is
Shunyata.

JASLEEN DHAMIJA
NEW DELHI

SLEEN DHAMIJA

leen Dhamija is known internationally as a
losopher of living cultural traditions and an
ortant contributor to the holistic approach to
io-cultural and economic development. She has
rked and researched in India and with United
ions in Iran, Middle East, Asia, South East Asia, as
l as with 21 countries in Africa. Her main speciality
istory of textiles and costumes.

he was awarded Hill Professorship by the
versity of Minnesota for her work on Textiles. She
s worked at the Faculty National Institute of Fashion
hnology, New Delhi, teaching History of Indian
tiles and Costumes and has been a Visiting Fellow,
ional Institute of Design. Resident Scholar of Art
leges in University of Canberra, Sydney and
llongon.

he has organized seminars on textile history,
tumes, draping and wrapping. Has lectured on
tiles in Museums in India, Europe, UK, USA, Japan,
stralia and South East Asia.

From 1965 over a dozen publications have been
tten by her on subjects such as Indian textiles,
broidery, carpets, handwoven fabrics of India,
ven silks, patola, textiles of Andhra etc. Her latest
*Woven Magic: The Affinity between Indian and
onesian Textiles.*

JNESCO has appointed her as President of Jury of
an Award for creativity in textile over the last
ple of years.

Textile, Volume 1, Issue 2, p. 157
Reprints available directly from the Publishers.
Photocopying permitted by licence only.
© 2003 Berg. Printed in the United Kingdom.

Chinese Whispers:
Variations on Textile

Abstract

This article extends the meaning of *textile* to explore its relation to the cinematic screen, drawing on the writings of Gilles Deleuze, Julia Kristeva, and others. Reading the textured surfaces of Zhang Yimou's *Ju Dou*, a beautiful Chinese film set in a fabric-dying factory, the Baroque scenographies of Piranesi, Watteau's *fêtes galantes*, and Vivienne Westwood's fashion designs, it considers appearance through speech, gesture, and the body adorned or abused and damaged by craft and labor. In thinking through the *textile screen*, and observing processes running in and between networks of texts, it makes a theoretical gesture toward the utopian political possibilities of *textile* as an acoustic screen in which disparate voices interact.

⋯S GRAY

⋯ Gray is researching a Ph.D. in History of Art at the
⋯artment of Historical and Cultural Studies,
⋯dsmiths College, University of London. She has
⋯ked as an editor for a number of art book
⋯lishers.

Textile, Volume 1, Issue 2, pp. 158–173
Reprints available directly from the Publishers.
Photocopying permitted by licence only.
© 2003 Berg. Printed in the United Kingdom.

Chinese Whispers: Variations on Textile

Textile, texture, textuality, tissue. Emerging in this game of Chinese whispers are variations on the word *textile*. Arcane networks of signification come to the fore, shifting the frames through which to analyze the cinematic screen. This article proposes that the cinematic screen can be seen to be somehow *textile*, and that this changes the meaning of *textile* so that it comes to inhabit the spaces of the cinematic. It places into exploratory relation a series of readings. Of *Ju Dou* (1989), an exquisitely beautiful Chinese film by Zhang Yimou that is a story of love and cruelty, but is also about cloth making and the making of the meaning of cloth.[1] Of Piranesi's *Carceri* etchings (1760); and of Watteau's *Cythera* paintings, a version of which inspired the dandyified and arcadian figures in Vivienne Westwood's fashion collections. To recite the word *textile*, to badger it, and to unravel its etymological links, the article poses a constellation of utopian and dystopian visions, peopled with subjects that attempt a self-articulation that is resistant to dominant symbolic orders.

Threading between these different works is a concern with the metaphor of social fabric and with notions of textuality as a social network, elaborated with references to Barthes's early writings on the *Text* and Deleuzian notions of the perceptual "fold." This is recognized in a Baroque "textile model of the kind implied by garments" that reconfigures the relations between subjects and objects through the textures folded into and between them, and into their unique perceptions.[2] Thinking through the *textile screen* means to observe processes running in and between networks of texts, reading textually the surfaces of voices, bodies, and material visual culture. The pursuit of an extended meaning for *textile* opens up processes of mutual elucidation that make a theoretical gesture toward an allegorical status for cinematic space relating to the formation of spheres of social interaction. The *textile screen* may be conceived as the condition for the emergence of novel and resistant modes of civic appearance. In structuring multiple and simultaneous meanings for the screen as a psychic mechanism of perception and as multiform surfaces upon which projections are laid out, it becomes apparent that its *textile* surface filters the seeming chaos of matter into tentative figures of the political, utopian "not-yet-conscious."

Arcane Machinery

Zhang Yimou's film *Ju Dou* is set in a remote village in China in 1920 in a fabric-dying factory, oppressively governed by patriarchal Confucian familial law and ancestor worship. Only passing reference is made to the violent social upheavals taking place throughout China at that time, which the village itself seems touched by.[3] Between the high alls that enclose the dark urtyard, drapes of textile are hung ove pools of dye on frames that e up above the dusty wooden achinery (Figure 1). It is owned by e aged Jinshan, a brutal man who rtures his young wife Ju Dou until e turns for love and sympathy to s adopted nephew Tienqing. The ctory is where wet cloth has its mbolic colors imposed upon it, for e as banners in ceremonies that rform and reinforce the social erarchy. The despotic rule rsonified by Jinshan extends into the labyrinthine village around the factory through a clan of elders and gossiping villagers who dictate the lives of Ju Dou and Tienqing even after Jinshan's death. In this patriarchal structure Ju Dou is, as a woman, the nomadic element in the social fabric. Her inclusion within the familial structure marks the beginning of the story, and it is through her struggle to find private happiness and act out her desires that the drama unfolds. Her role in the story is, as in Kristeva's words in *On Chinese Women*, "of negation, of change, of movement."[4]

In the presence of others we barely hear Ju Dou's voice, and her gestures merely perform docile submission. Only in the realm of familial intimacy does her fullness make its appearance—in turns yearning, coquettish, passionate or desperate with rage and despair. It is in the movements of her body, her laughter, and the modulations in her voice, from expressing tender excitement on learning she is pregnant by Tienqing to spitting words of vociferous contempt for Jinshan, that Ju Dou communicates forbidden and secret desires, and

gure 1
terior of the fabric-dying factory, *Ju Dou*.

through which, in the confines of the factory, she disrupts the order of patriarchy. She begins her seduction of Tienqing, who at first only spies on her bathing in secret, by turning her naked body toward him. Her bruised and battered skin is only faintly erotic, rather it protests against her torture by Jinshang and confides to Tienqing a wish for sympathy and love (Figure 2). A brief period of happiness for the couple following the paralysis that renders Jinshan temporarily powerless is suddenly broken when Ju Dou and Tienqing's illegitimate son, Tienbai, whom they thought to be mute, utters the word "father" to Jinshan. He thereby takes on the patriarchal role of persecutor and confirms his legitimacy as master the factory. Following the accident drowning of Jinshan, the clan elde force Ju Dou and Tienqing to make physically grueling performance during the funeral procession as a test of their loyalty to the official lineage. As the procession advanc amid swirling banners of white clo with Chinese characters emblazoned upon them, they mus repeatedly throw themselves unde Jinshan's coffin on which Tienbai i seated swaddled in robes as sole heir (Figure 3).

The factory, with its machinery, pools of dye and drapes of cloth, i full of dangers—the characters

Figure 2
Ju Dou and Tienqing, *Ju Dou*.

peatedly get tangled in the fabric, eir bodies become battered and uised by the machinery, and the ools of dye discolor the hands that rk the cloth. It functions as a aterial extension of the restrictive cial fabric to which all actions are d. Indeed, it is with cloth that Ju u is bound by Jinshan as he rtures her, and with pieces of rope at he is hoisted to the upper floor a barrel after his paralysis. shan's eventually drowning is used by Tienbai who, pulling him ong with a piece of string, advertently tips his barrel into a

pool of dye. The factory appears to be ancient and untouched by time. Yet the decrepit structure is also ripe for demolition, its frailty confirmed as the machinery spirals out of control when, in the first act of spontaneous love-making, Ju Dou kicks the structure into motion and drapes tumble down around her into the vats of dye.

How might figures in *Ju Dou*, momentarily caught in shafts of light, prompt a thinking of how the cinematic screen itself is *textile*? At certain moments in the film, when Tienqing watches Ju Dou at her

labor perched on the frames above, sunlight falls between drapes of yellow and red fabric, capturing an image of her face in the midst, its contours wrapped in light. The image is fleeting, indistinct. At such points, strips of light and textile become indistinguishable in their interplay, bringing to prominence the very texture of the cinematic screen. In these moments of appearance when the *textile screen* is most apparent, light breaks through obscurity to illuminate the desire that courses between two individuals who

gure 3
e funeral procession, *Ju Dou*.

cannot receive recognition as partners in love.

Might the screen be conceived not as a hard, reflective mirror, but as a *textile* surface, porous even when densely knit? This is a screen that, like a filter, allows something—an event, an object—to issue forth and take form from a chaos of multiplicity. In his reading of Leibniz and the Baroque, Deleuze identifies a conception of matter, echoed in current understanding of particle physics, as containing infinite heterogeneous parts folded into unique singularities. This plurality comes to us as:

> . . . *[m]icroperceptions or representatives of the world . . . little folds that unravel in every direction, folds in folds, over folds, following folds . . . And these are minute, obscure, confused perceptions that make up our macroperceptions, our conscious, clear, and distinct apperceptions.*[5]

Baroque painting, in which the contours of forms become apparent in the shafts of light that emerge from the canvas ground of dark chiaroscuro, serves for Deleuze as an analogy for the process by which conscious perceptions take form. Yet think also how the microsounds that make up notes and chords in music are only now becoming apparent to human consciousness through visual technologies that smear grains of sound upon the computer screen, enabling composition through microscopic variations that effect the macroscopic perception of music. Variations in the minute grains filter up to the surface like the movement of air from lower to upper floors in Baroque architecture.

Perception is "hallucinatory" because it has no object, instead a "screen intervenes" that brings order to seeming chaos, and it is through the "haze of dust without objects that the figures [of conscious perception] themselves raise up from the depths, and fall back again, but with time enough to be seen for an instant."[6] If, as Deleuze asserts, perception is the affective illusion of a unique subject that comes into being at a "point of view," the subject at this site or position is not a "pregiven or defined" entity, but comes into relation with a new kind of object in flux, the "objectile" that "assumes place in a continuum by variation." And because perception begins at the "point of view" of the subject, the manner in which hallucinatory microperceptions are folded into figures, there are always "prehensions" to the perception that gives it unity. These are the "echoes, reflections, traces, prismatic deformations, perspective, thresholds, folds" that anticipate psychic life. What the screen filters through is not merely that which is conditioned by the subject's point of view, but that which is a "virtual" possibility in the world.[8] The cinematic screen is not a window, but a surface grid on which a projection is laid out. The figures and configurations become so many different ways in which a "'flat projection' is mapped out." Upon this textile surface "it is the objectile that now declines or describes relations of curves . . . This objectile or projection resembles an unfolding."[9] There are always variations to come on the xtile surface, in which a unique ?ference is folded. Fold after fold.

The "threshold" of the screen is e beginning of a movement within e subject from "seeing to reading, im event of the thing . . . to edicate of the notion or concept." ough perception is always endered unstable" by the ricklings" of microperceptions, it vertheless is the process through iich the subject makes a selection d determines what is "notable or markable."[10] Reading becomes a id of reasonable interaction, in iich neither subject nor object are ed, but constantly in flux and ded into one another. Writing ght then be seen as an action of ganizing objects that are bjectively remarkable upon a ane visible from the "point of iw." Yet this perspective is not able—it aspires to draw out clarity im obscurity but must always counter other singularities. ibniz's notion is that, as in music, ere can be a plural "harmony" of igularities that meet in vibration, rceive one another and emselves, and create a world. The indition of public life is that the bject cannot produce its own ccords," but acting in a crowd ust:

. . follow the lines of melody.
The two begin to fuse a sort of
diagonal, where the monads
penetrate each other, are
modified, inseparable from the
groups of prehension that carry
them along and make up as
many transitory captures.[11]

How to read and write "who" ther than "what" a person is? How align oneself with the "marginal

speech" at the fringes of "capitalist monotheistic fabric" that embodies desires foreign and disruptive to the status quo, without, as Kristeva cautions in her attempts to "write" Chinese women, imposing one's own projections.[12] To read and to write—can it be to courteously inhabit other voices as well as one's own, and to give something of oneself with generosity? This perhaps is the beginning of an ethics of forming an argument, of its nature partial, in flux and in interaction with other texts that speak and listen to one another.

Civilitas

Ju Dou fights an anachronistic social structure, driven by a desire that can find no outlet in existing social forms. Images of the dusty factory, lit from above by sunlight that falls through the drapes of textile, provide a figure of arcane machinery through which to read the fantastical prison etchings of Piranesi (Figure 4). Mapping such cinematic textures in *Ju Dou* over the very contrasts of light and dark chiaroscuro through which the architectural structures take form in the *Carceri* extends the textile screen from the cinematic through to the surfaces of Baroque scenography. In this configuration the labyrinth is a scene of despotism, of spies, and minotaural terror. As an adolescent the bullish Tienbai rampages through the narrow streets of the village, terrorizing anyone who casts doubt on his parentage. In the *Carceri* the individual is reduced to powerlessness. The only human figures are tiny bodies caught alone within macabre machines of torture, and the insignias visible in the

shadows of labyrinthine structures are evidently no guarantors of republican justice, but emblems of imperial tyranny (Figure 5).

It has been argued that the spectator is "implicated" in Piranesi's dystopic Baroque vision, drawn in to reconfigure the fragments of architectural construction in a puzzle that "proves to be unsolvable."[13] He or she participates in the performance only to discover the relative futility of his/her readings, confronted by a structure that, though decaying, is monolithic and offers no alternative. In these Baroque sceneographies the balance of classical architecture is indeed set spiraling. His earlier *Pianta di ampio magnifico collegio* (Plan of a magnificent college, 1750; Figure 6) is formed around a central spiral staircase, expanding outwards through ever-enlarging concentric structures. While aspiring to provide a utopian arena for social interaction, this model demonstrates a process of extension to the periphery and dialogue between divergent parts that undoes the pretensions to centrality that the project seems to commence with. The ideal viewing position of the sovereign subject, projected out of the classical picture plane by single point perspective, is left radically indeterminate.

Yet the very act of reading through the cinematic *textile screen* onto the textured surface of these scenographies suggests a transformative engagement rather than "implication," with its associations with guilt-ridden collusion. The constant gliding movement of textuality—always a "production," "practice" or "play" in the field of the signifier—refuses

Figure 4
Giovanbattista Piranesi, *Carceri*, plate VII.
Etching, 55 × 41 cm. In G. Piranesi,
Carceri d'invenzione, c. 1761.

to be transfixed by sublime visions of despotism. Textuality is a *textile* surface that is constantly made and remade through the interaction of texts with each other and with the subjects that read and, at the same time, write them. As in the Deleuzian figure of the fold, subjects come into being in their interaction with matter that is continually in flux. Through variation, manners and styles are constantly folded into each other and unraveled into something new. In this movement of folding and unfolding, styles extend beyond the frames of disciplines, to produce an "interlocking of frames of which each is exceeded by a matter that moves through it."[14] In his analysis of cinema, Deleuze posits the screen as the "frame of frames,"[15] the "dovetailing" of frames being the means through which disparate

Figure 5
Giovanbattista Piranesi, *Carceri*, plate II.
Etching, 55.5 × 42 cm. In G. Piranesi,
Carceri d'invenzione, c. 1761.

arts of the moving image are separated but also converge and are reunited."[16] The cinematic frame finds its analogue in the information system rather than in linguistics in that the flux of matter within the frame tends toward "saturation" or "rarefaction."[17] There may be a multiplication of simultaneous scenes, or a single object can momentarily loom into presence. The cinematic *textile screen* is thus

the surface upon which relations are established between painting, sculpture, architecture, and city planning through extension of matter that forms "a universal theatre that includes air and earth, and even fire and water," drawing the spectator "into this very performance."[18]

This Baroque theater is an ever-shifting city space where the political, as Hannah Arendt

conceived it, is embodied, not in the institutions of governance, but in the fleeting realm of human action. The "web" of human relationships is the tissue in which individuals make an "appearance," their bodily actions and speech being the only means through which it is revealed "who" rather than "what" a person is as a distinct and unique human being.[19] The "space of appearance" is thus not the same as the

Figure 6
Giovanbattista Piranesi, *Pianta di ampio
magnifico collegio* (Plan of a magnificent
college). Etching, 61 × 45 cm. In G.
Piranesi, *Opere varie*, 1750.

monumental and enduring
architectural constructions with
which neoclassical architecture
sought to build an enclave for
civilized social interaction. Instead it
is produced in the very speaking
and acting of human beings in their
"sheer human togetherness;"[20] it is
the temporary stage of a continual
process of "enacting" that accrues
meaning only in retrospect, in the
telling of the story of a life. The
capacity of individuals to act and

thereby reveal and insert
themselves into the temporal scene
thus always emerges through the
tissue or network of social relations
In Kristeva this is formed from the
"coordinates" of "ranks of ancestor
and future generations," and
involves a process of learning the
"symbolic function." This is a
"system of signs (first, rhythmic an
intonational differences, then
signified/signifer) organized into
logico-syntactic structures whose

al is to accredit social mmunication as exchange of rified pleasure."[21]

However, Arendt's notions of ction" and "the space of pearance" open up possibilities reading modes of speech, acts, stures, and accoutrements as ns of resistance on the fringes of tablished symbolic codes. hough Kristeva emphasizes the mbolic social codes through ich subjectivity makes its esence, Arendt's web or tissue is rmed from the action and speech at connects people—it is a ubjective in-between" that is rely tangible, and that is the eans through which, ironically in heer togetherness," difference akes an appearance.[22] In "Le grain la voix" Barthes describes the und of a song having a surface at "papers over" the body of the nger.[23] With the increasing onopoly of certain modes of nging and expression, gnification comes to suffocate the rcharge of affectivity—vocal stures are reduced to the signs of starlet's "personality," and the uissance or erotic rapport perienced in the encounter tween listener and singer into a ded emotion.[24] His writing on the xtuality of music advocates tending to the appearance of bjectivity through speech, sture, and the body adorned, used and damaged by craft and bor. To focus on textures or the rain" of the voice, costume, and ushstroke, is to seek out the uances of "significance" that ade or unravel codification in isting symbolic forms. Matter ws through the multiform frames the *textile screen* like expanding

and contracting rivulets, suggesting that the social arena of the Baroque stage is formed from mobile and interlinking surfaces upon which the faintest ripple subtly modifies the whole. And in Baroque drama the political status of the allegorical gesture comes to the fore—as a means in the despotic social arena of the court of masking subversion by an ambiguous articulation that recites the august figures of mythology. Beyond the courtly theater in the spaces of the city, cloth makes the most immediate and incendiary transformation of surface meaning as, at moments of upheaval, at the festival or the demonstration, streets flame with a flurry of banners and flags.

In the official ceremonies in *Ju Dou*, bodies are swaddled with fabric that symbolically wraps them into the social hierarchy. Yet with abstract shots in which light shines through layers of fabric, the film suggests ways in which cloth comes to evoke more nuanced and complex meanings. The supple wet cloth that hangs to dry is yet to have its meaning fixed—it easily falls from its frames in fluid cascades to become a pantheistic figure for erotic ecstasy. In Deleuze's reading of Baroque costume, fabric becomes an envelope that extends the body and imbues it with spiritual force. For Deleuze, the "distending waves" of fabric in Baroque costume of the seventeenth century overwhelm the body beneath with an infinity of tiny pleats and ornate ribbons, flowing coats, and exaggerated flaps. Cloth demonstrates "autonomy" from the human subject. In its representation in painting drapes of fabric invade the surface, rupturing the symmetry

of Renaissance perspective. These billowing, radiating folds act as "go-betweens" that flow between the body and clothing so that they take on an expressive force that in turn molds the "inner surfaces" of the body. Baroque sculpture then becomes an art of textures rather than structures, as in Bernini's figures, where marble "seizes and bears to infinity folds that cannot be explained by the body, but by a spiritual adventure that can set the body ablaze."[25]

The Baroque tendency to repeat and contort shapes and textures is evident in the contemporary designs of Vivienne Westwood, who recites the textile statements of seventeenth- and eighteenth-century costume in her own singular garments. She has even played with the conceit of molding wet drapery to the body, a technique adopted to mimic the shapes of classical sculpture. Her costumes, as she admitted in the television series *Painted Ladies*, walk a tightrope, aspiring to embody "nobility," "civility" and "seduction" at the risk of falling into the ridiculous. The collection "Voyage to Cythera", for instance, takes inspiration from the tradition of "English tailoring," but also from the erotic fantasy of Arcadian aristocratic leisure depicted by Watteau. With his second *Cythera* painting, *Pilgrimage to Cythera* (1717) (Figure 7), he sought to gain admittance to the Académie, elevating his signature pictorial subject of the *fête galante* to the status of mythological allegory. The couples in the painting are dressed either in aristocratic or rustic costume in current and past styles, and wear the short capes and carry the staffs of pilgrims. The garments suggest the timelessness of theatrical allegory, yet the painting does not make reference to established iconography, and, as Posner suggests, "does not bear analysis as a story or as a logical allegorical construction."[26] The viewer is left tantalizingly uncertain even as to whether the couples are about to embark for Cythera or have in fact already arrived. The invitation to participate in reading this enchanted image stems from the delicate gestures of gallant lovers rather than from visual tropes with clear symbolic meaning.

From the eighteenth century techniques of tailoring were developed to contort the male body through structure, cutting coats with a "dynamic flourish" aimed at expressing character rather than, as in men's suits today, shaping the perfect body. For Westwood's 1989 collection, female models were squeezed into tailored jackets and clinging tights that mimicked men's breeches, with flirtatious fig leaves placed upon the groin. In her 1996 show a corset distorted the upper body of one male model, so that he could display the "Martyr to Love" jacket, which had layers of pearls and sequins that replicated the muscular torso of a nude Greek statue, extending the surface of the body in undulating layers to the point of camp whimsy. Adorning the body comes to involve a verbose exaggeration of natural contours that inflicts pain through craft rather than labor, for the sake of a luxurious quip. Through every technique of artifice, Westwood

Figure 7
Antoine Watteau, *Pilgrimage to Cythera*, 1717. Oil on canvas, 129 × 193 cm. Musée du Louvre, Paris.

shes fashion toward expressing a
allenge to conformity, an anarchic
lividualism that also recites the
stures and forms of twilight
tism. Her figures are like dandies
o strut aloof from the crowd in a
ded cage.

Yet, if Westwood's seducers and
rtyrs stand alone, what connects
tteau's paintings to *Ju Dou* is the
eoccupation with lovers and their
sh for escape from the world and
m public scrutiny. Ju Dou is finally
ven to suicide by burning down
e very structure of the prison–
tory that contains her. The film
ds with the literal destruction of
e stage of action, which has
come a prison. Kristeva recounts
it in the 1920s the young Mao
w in the Chinese feminist
vement a "radical means of
nsforming society," identifying in
e rash of suicides by young
men a kind of passive "activism,"
e notion of which Kristeva
jectures may be inflected with
ddhist doctrine. Mao saw that,

. . liberalism and the feminist
novement are beginning to draw
onverts among the great mass
f women, but the social
tructure is not prepared. The
oung rebels, then having
ommitted themselves to far-
eaching ideals of emancipation
ith no concrete means of
ealizing them, find themselves
ubject to the violent disapproval
f those around them, and
esperately seek an end to their
roblems by putting an end to
eir lives.[27]

Activism is reconfigured here,
ggesting that outside the Western
adigms of emancipation through

individualism there are ways in
which we might read certain actions
or the "enacting" of the body within
the social as a form of activism that
has not yet taken conscious form.

Watteau's first *Cythera* painting
(*c.* 1709) depicts a stage set—the
figures are static and formal, and
skies and landscape are neutral.[28]
However, in the second version
rococo flourishes emerge as the
brushwork frees itself, and delicate
pinks and blues imbue the painting
with dulcet tones. Here too,
garments are puffed up with folds
and ruffles of lace that rise up
beneath the hems of gowns and the
sleeves of coats. For Ernst Bloch, the
brushwork and textures of light in
the second Paris version (1717)
represented a "wish-landscape" in
its "anticipation of desire" to reach
happiness in the night of the island
of love.[29] The very indistinctness of
the contours of the landscape in
veils of dusk holds the image in a
moment of hope. In contrast, the
third version (1720) was for Bloch
already too "bijou." With its
saccharine colors and elaborate
rendering of putti circling the boat's
sail, Cythera "already seems to have
been reached."[30] Bloch posits a
"utopian function" for art that
becomes apparent to the reader in
the act of nuanced attention to such
variations in form and tone, the
spectator transforming him or
herself into a participant through
the affective interaction between
subjects and texts. Resistance to
the status quo driven by desire only
emerges into consciousness
through some figure in a wishful
daydream. As in the *Pilgrimage to
Cythera*, "anticipatory illumination"
of "not-yet-conscious" wishes for
the future may be emitted in the

textures and forms of artworks. The
utopic for Bloch is found in the
minutiae of psychic and material
processes that have not yet been
integrated within the prevailing
social framework. Utopias instead
begin to take form in the hazy and
indistinct textures of visual and
literary texts, at the fringes that
escape rigid signification.

Figures without Bodies

Textile extends the metaphor of
cinematic space beyond notions of
its being an ideological apparatus
that merely perpetuates an arcane
social machine. It attempts to give
recognition to resistance only
manifested in gestures, sounds and
textures that voice desires for
possibilities not yet signified in the
social. Power, as Arendt conceived
it, resides solely as a possibility
whenever people come together—it
is not the same as force, and it
disappears as the crowd disperses.
Kristeva draws attention to the
"other scene" so hard to "write," of
sexual difference, the family, the
bedchamber, kept hidden from the
directed forms of social and political
participation and not so easily
"socialized" into writing. These are
desires rarely spoken of, but
"written in gestures and with
paintbrushes."[31] Here, she says,

one might realize the necessity
for creating a society where
power is active, but not
symbolized by anyone... man
and woman, men and women,
exercising it only to criticize it,
. . . move it . . . if each individual
. . . took it upon himself to
remake it with his/her practice,
in his/her discussions with
others, in each individual act, in

*each concrete moment. A
utopia?³²*

This is a notion of utopia not as the ideal "no-where" of classical idealism, but as Deleuze and Guattari insist, a "now-here." A political and creative utopia of continual remaking:

*Utopia does not split off from
infinite movement:
etymologically it stands for
absolute deterritorialization but
always at the critical point at
which it is connected with the
present relative milieu, and
especially with the forces stifled
by this milieu.³³*

Textile can be understood as both the textured surface upon which subjects come into being at a "point of view," and as the screen in which objects take their perceived form. Divergent voices weave a brecciated mobile surface—an acoustic *textile screen*, upon which the inscription of difference is the condition of its dissonant harmony. The imagining of new subjectivities and alternative social milieux takes place on the fringes of the textile screen and in its subterranean layers, at the points of variation, of its fraying and its luxurious excess. Here future modes of resistance are projected like flashes of light in the dark shuttling of desire between subjects and objects. Ripple, swirl, unfurl . . .

Notes

1. *Ju Dou* was initially banned in China for several years. According to Jenny Kwok Wah Lau, this was not due to erotic explicitness but because the authorities interpreted the film as, at best, a negative portrayal of China, or, at worst, a critique of the current regime. Jenny Kwok Wah Lau, "Judou—A Hermeneutical Reading of Cross-cultural Cinema," in *Film Quarterly*, 45(2), Winter 1991/9

2. Gilles Deleuze, The Fold: Leibniz and the Baroque (London: Althone Press, 1993), p. 121.

3. The Manchu dynasty fell in 19 China was proclaimed a republic in 1912 under Sun Yat-sen. Sun's Kuomintang (Nationalist Party) attempted reunite China from conflict between regional warlords. The Chinese Communist Party (CCP was founded in 1921. CCP members such as Mao Tse-Tung and others organized strikes and unions throughout the 1920s, and formed an alliance with the Kuomintang in 1924 fight the Japanese. The Kuomintang under Chiang Kai shek drove the CCP underground after liberation Shanghai.

4. Julia Kristeva, *About Chinese Women* (London: Marion Boyars, 1977), p. 115.

5. Deleuze, The Fold, p. 86.

6. *Ibid.*, p. 94.

7. *Ibid.*, p. 19.

8. *Ibid.*, p. 26.

9. *Ibid.*, pp. 20–1.

10. *Ibid.*, p. 86.

11. *Ibid.*, p. 137.

12. Kristeva, *About Chinese Women* pp. 13–16.

13. May Sekler, cited in Manfredo Tarfuri, *The Sphere and the Labyrinth: Avant-Gardes and Architecture from Piranesi to t 1970s* (Cambridge, MA: MIT Press, 1987), p. 26.

Ibid., p. 123.

Gilles Deleuze, *Cinema 1: The Movement-Image*, trans. Hugh Tomlinson and Barbara Habberjam (London: Althone Press, 1986), p. 14.

Ibid., p. 15.

Ibid., p. 12.

Deleuze, *The Fold*, p. 124.

Hannah Arendt, *The Human Condition* (Chicago, IL: University of Chicago Press, 1958), p. 179.

Ibid., p. 180.

Kristeva, *About Chinese Women*, pp. 30–1.

Hannah Arendt, *The Human Condition*, pp. 182–3.

The phrase is: "comme si une meme peau tapissait la chair interieure de l'executant et la musique qu'il chante." Roland Barthes, "Le grain de la voix," in *L'ovie et l'obtus: Essais critiques III* (Paris: Editions du Seuil, 1982), p. 238.

Ibid., p. 244.

Deleuze, *The Fold*, p. 122.

Donald Posner, *Antoine Watteau* (London: Weidenfeld & Nicolson, 1984), p. 192.

Cited in Kristeva, *About Chinese Women*, p. 109.

Posner notes that a pilgrimage to Cythera was acted out or mentioned several times on the theatrical stage in Paris between 1713 and 1716. Posner, *Antoine Watteau*, p. 187.

Ernst Bloch, "The Representation of Wish-Landscapes in Painting, Opera and Poetry," in *The Utopian Function of Art and Literature: Selected Essays*, trans. Jack Zipes and Frank Mecklenburg (Cambridge MA: MIT Press, 1996), pp. 278–86.

30. *Ibid.*, p. 182.

31. *Ibid.*, p. 159.

32. *Ibid.*, p. 200.

33. Gilles Deleuze and Felix Guattari, *What is Philosophy?*, trans. Hugh Tomlinson and Graham Burchill (London and New York: Verso, 1994), pp. 99–100.

Filmography

Ju Dou (1989), directed by Zhang Yimou; written by Liu Heng.

Without Walls: Painted Ladies (1996), directed by Gordon Swire; produced by Cynthia Kin; written and presented by Vivienne Westwood.

Bibliography

Arendt, Hannah. 1958. *The Human Condition*. London: University of Chicago Press.

Barthes, Roland. 1982. "Le grain de la voix." In *L'ovie et obtus: Essais critiques III*. Paris: Editions du Seuil.

——. 1986. "From Work to Text." In *The Rustle of Language*, trans. Richard Howard. Oxford: Basil Blackwell.

Benjamin, Walter. 1977. *The Origin of German Tragic Drama*, trans. John Osborne. London: NLB.

——. 1999. *Illuminations*. London: Verso.

Bloch, Ernst. 1996. *The Utopian Function of Art and Literature: Selected Essays*. Cambridge MA: MIT Press.

Deleuze, Gilles. 1986. *Cinema 1: The Movement-Image*, trans. Hugh Tomlinson and Barbara Habberjam. London: Althone Press.

——, *The Fold: Liebniz and the Baroque*. (London: Althone Press, 1993).

—— and Felix Guattari. 1994. *What is Philosophy?*, trans. Hugh Tomlinson and Graham Burchill. London and New York: Verso.

Kristeva, Julia. 1997. *About Chinese Women*. London: Marion Boyars.

Kwok Wah Lau, Jenny. 1991/92. '*Judou* – A Hermeneutical Reading of Cross-cultural Cinema." *Film Quarterly* 45(2), Winter 1991/92, 2–10.

Posner, Donald. 1984. *Antoine Watteau*. London: Weidenfeld & Nicolson.

Roads, Curtis. 2001. *Microsound*. Cambridge, MA: MIT Press.

Tarfuri, Manfredo. 1987. *The Sphere and the Labyrinth: Avant-Gardes and Architecture from Piranesi to the 1970s*. Cambridge MA: MIT Press.

Embroidering the Nation

Abstract

This paper discusses the sixteen-metre long embroidery, worked by members of the Embroiderers' Guild throughout Australia, to a design by Kay Lawrence, for the Great Hall in Australia's new Parliament House opened in Canberra in 1988. The building itself generates a discourse of land and landscape to express national identity, making assumptions about Australia's past and present and the functioning of parliamentary democracy many of which are open to question. The design brief directed that the embroidery focus on the settlement of the land and Kay Lawrence explores both positive and negative aspects of this theme, challenging ideological assumptions held by many Australians. The paper examines the embroidery's context in Parliament House and the negotiations that took place between designer and embroiderers with regard to the content and execution of the work.

ROTHY JONES

othy Jones, formerly an Associate Professor in the
ish Department of the Unifersity of Wollongong,
tralia, is now an honorary fellow of the University.
has published widely in the field of postcolonial
ng, focussing particularly on women's writing.
has also published a number of papers on the
tionship between textiles and literature and is
ently engaged in a research project with
eagues from the University of Wollongong on
oric(ation)s of the Postcolonial" which examines
tionships between textiles, trade and literary
.

Textile, Volume 1, Issue 2, pp. 174–194
Reprints available directly from the Publishers.

Embroidering the Nation

Introduction

The embroidery commissioned for the east gallery of the Great Hall in Australia's new Parliament House, opened in 1988, represents a vision of Australia over a period prior to white settlement until 1900, helping constitute that non-verbal commentary about people, place, and nationhood conveyed by the building as a whole. In 1980 Dorothy Hyslop first suggested creating the embroidery to fellow members of the Australian Capital Territory (ACT) Embroiderers' Guild as a project which Guild members throughout Australia could complete as a gift to the nation.[1] Although many of the embroiderers, both in the ACT and beyond, were dismayed at the magnitude of the task and initially hesitant to undertake it, Mrs Hyslop's vision, energy and commitment helped win them over and were largely responsible for the project proceeding so effectively to its eventual fruition. Her proposal was put to the Joint House Standing Committee of the new Parliament House and accepted, with the Parliament House Embroidery Committee set up in the ACT on 27 October 1980 and convened by Dorothy Hyslop. It was decided that the embroidery should be long and narrow so it could be divided into eight panels to be worked separately by guild members in each of the six States and the two Territories. A design competition was announced in 1983 and South Australian artist Kay Lawrence's entry was accepted unanimously by the Art Advisory Committee of the Crafts Board of the Australia Council in June 1984.[2] After discussion between embroiderers and architects' representatives, it was decided to place the completed work in the first-floor gallery of the Great Hall, a monumental space devoted to the concept of "the land." Although the embroidery develops its own theme, it gathers added meaning and resonance from its location in a central site of Australian politics.

Political and Topographical Contexts

Political places both reflect and help create the myth of nation, demonstrating not only "architectural conventions of the day," but also "the conscious preferences of those in power at the time," along with "underlying characteristics of the prevailing system of political authority."[3] As time passes, state mythologies crystallize and their meanings become ever more clearly apparent as, for example, in Renaissance Venice, where official figurations by innumerable artists helped construct the state itself as a work of art.[4] Although the architect of Australia's new Parliament House, Romaldo Giurgola, of Mitchell, Giurgola and Thorpe, may have sought to revive a Renaissance idea (and parts of the building carry Renaissance echoes),[5] no seat of government built in a post-Enlightenment, postmodern age can draw so directly on the rich blend of Christian, humanist, and classical tradition characterizing the political places of the Venetian republic. Moreover, the meanings inherent in so recent a building are still fluctuating and uncertain. Australia's Parliament House, completed and opened in 1988, seeks to celebrate the virtues of democracy while, in design and ornamentation, it looks to the land itself for inspiration, authority and validation. Giurgola was expected to fit in with US designer Walter Burley Griffin's city plan for Canberra, devised in the early twentieth century, even though this was only partially realized. Griffin had intended that the legislature should be built on Camp Hill, overlooked by Capital Hill for which he planned a "Capitol" building for public assembly and housing archives. The respective placing of these two buildings was to signify parliament's democratic subordination to the people. Although Capital Hill became the chosen site for Australia's new Parliament House, the building is set into the hill so it is possible to walk over its grass-covered summit, allowing people to stand directly above their elected representatives.

Some commentators, however, observing the demarcation between areas for public display and those requiring access by security pass, question how far the building's structure represents democratic ideals with key centers of parliamentary power, like the cabinet room, deeply buried—"a room without windows, a box within a box, a bunker isolated from the outside world."[6]

New Parliament House, Canberra, an architectural

complex entirely geared to the visitor, the spectator, hygienically sealing off the actual business of politics from its spectacle. This because New Parliament House envisages politics in contemporary terms, as image-making, PR, in short, virtuality.[7]

Philip Drew, noting how white Australians have seized upon the geographical feature Ayers Rock (Uluru) located near Alice Springs as a centric symbol, compares this natural dome with the one reconstituted above new Parliament House. "You could say it is a kind of neat, lawn-covered suburban version of Ayers Rock." The grassy covering, however, hides what is really happening below. "Hence the New Parliament's natural dome suggests concealment and hidden power."[8]

Land, landscape, and nationalism have long been associated. "National identity . . . would lose most of its ferocious enchantment without the mystique of a particular landscape tradition: its topography mapped, elaborated, and enriched as a homeland."[9] Ivor Indyk notes how, despite all its statements about power, Parliament House seeks to subsume political activity within an insistent discourse of Australian land and landscape and that this is particularly notable at those "hot" points "where paths meet, where there is likely to be action or debate, where decisions are to be taken."[10] The dominance of landscape imagery and allusion in Parliament House suggests the building and its activities are sanctioned by Nature itself eliding uncomfortable awareness of how

modern Australia came into being through the conquest and dispossession of its original inhabitants. The land was seen to serve as a symbol of unification, something, it is implied, that all Australians have in common. Indyk suggests that "the land quite literally acts as a common ground upon which the representatives of opposed persuasions might meet: references to the Australian landscape will command unanimity where references of a specifically political or social nature may only produce discord or division."[11] Ironically, since 1988 (bicentenary of white settlement), rights to land and landownership have proved a particularly divisive issue in Australia, with the High Court Mabo decision, recognizing indigenous claims to land, in 1992, recent debates about black armband and white blindfold views of history, and current disputes over refugees entering the country.[12]

The land is certainly not common ground for all Australians, nor is it a neutral topos. As we observe landscape, it mingles with our myths and visions of it which, as Simon Schama says, have already become part of the scenery. "Landscapes are culture before they are nature; constructs of the imagination projected onto wood and water and rock".[13] Such mythologizing directs how the theme of the land has been incorporated into the structure of Parliament House. Visitors approach through the open forecourt, with its central mosaic, designed by Papunya artist Michael Tjackamarra and based on an Aboriginal sand painting signifying the gathering of the tribe, seen as representing "the ancient continent" through "the great antiquity of Aboriginal art, an embodiment in contemporary form of the world's oldest living culture, evolved over more than 40,000 years."[14] Movement into the building through a facade surmounted by the Australian coat of arms with the supporting emu and kangaroo portrayed in open x-ray technique, as in Aboriginal drawings, then into the foyer which "with its rich materials and elegant details represents old Europe and marks the arrival of Western culture,"[15] involves many historical and cultural assumptions, all open to debate and contestation.

The Great Hall, intended for official receptions and banquets, was designed to evoke the period of settlement in Australia's history, its extensive space intended "to correlate symbolically with the vastness of the land."[16] Flanking the entrance door, under glass, are four quotations from documents associated with European presence in Australia and raising, intentionally or not, some thorny issues associated with colonization. Cook's *Journals* offer a golden age/noble savage view of Aborigines.

> . . . in reality they are far happier than we Europeans; being wholly unacquainted not only with the superfluous but the necessary conveniences so much sought after in Europe, they are happy in not knowing the use of them. They live in a Tranquillity which is not disturb'd by the Inequality of Condition: the Earth and sea of their own accord furnishes them with all things necessary for life, they covet not Magnificent Houses, Household-stuff etc.[17]

Another quotation, from the 1787 royal instructions to Arthur Phillip, Australia's first Governor, is among the building's very few allusions to the country's convict origins. Phillip is granted authority to emancipate convicts, endowing them with land, considered to be at the crown's disposal—"To every male shall be granted 30 acres of land, and in case he shall be married, 20 acres more." A further quotation comes from W. C. Wentworth's 1853 speech in the Legislative Council of New South Wales urging a new State constitution and arguing the need to confer on the country "that large measure of freedom" which may give rise to "an ennobling and exalted patriotism" inspiring youth of future ages, if need be, to die for their country.

Finally comes a famous passage from Marcus Clarke's 1876 preface to Adam Lindsay Gordon's *Sea Spray and Drift Smoke*.

> In Australia alone is to be found the Grotesque, the Weird, the strange scribblings of nature learning how to write. Some see no beauty in our trees without shade, our flowers without perfume, our birds who cannot fly, and our beasts who have not yet learned to walk on all fours. But the dweller in the wilderness acknowledges the subtle charm of this fantastic land of monstrosities. He becomes familiar with the beauty of loneliness. Whispered to by the myriad tongues of the wilderness, he learns the language of the barren and the uncouth, and can read the hieroglyphs of the haggard gum-trees, blown into odd shapes,

istorted with fierce hot winds, or
ramped with cold nights, when
ie Southern Cross freezes in a
loudless sky of icy blue. The
hantasmagoria of that wild
reamland termed the Bush
nterprets itself, and the Poet of
ur desolation begins to
omprehend why free Esau loved
is heritage of desert sand better
uan the bountiful richness of
gypt.[18]

ese are surprising words to
counter when entering the "room
he land" suggesting, as they do,
:h uncertainty about home and
neland. For all the references to
abtle charm," "the beauty of
eliness," and Esau's preference
his desert heritage, the
scription is remarkably negative.
lace which is now home is
rtrayed as weirdly alien, uncanny,
heimlich. It has been argued that
ese melancholic views of a
unted landscape were prompted
awareness of the dispossession
d violence done to Aborigines as
ite settlers projected their
ubled consciences onto what
y saw around them.[19]
ntemporary Australians may
rceive the landscape differently,
d many still feel haunted by it.

nning and Design of the
broidery

y Lawrence's design for the
broidery involves many issues
sed directly or indirectly by the
otations at the Great Hall
orway. The design brief directed
it the work was to "examine the
cept of the Australian land and
impact upon the human values
d lives of its inhabitants through

the period of settlement from 1788–
1900" and that it should be an
integral part in the sequence of
artworks in Parliament House.[20]
Because, from the eighteenth
century on, embroidery has been
indissolubly linked with
stereotypical femininity and ideals
of domesticity, some have difficulty
in regarding it as an appropriate
medium for public or political
expression.[21] One early suggestion
from the architects' office was that,
instead of a pictorial embroidery,
the guilds might consider making a
large tablecloth for use on
ceremonial occasions. This was
firmly rejected by members who
wanted something for all to see
(PHE, 2). Dorothy Hyslop associates
the embroidery with a number of
commemorative embroideries
around the world, most particularly
the Bayeux Tapestry (which is in fact
an embroidery), narrating events
leading to the Battle of Hastings in
1066 and the triumph of William the
Conqueror.[22] This work is an
important reference point for the
Parliament House embroidery which
shares its long narrow shape, and
much else besides.

Although commissioned by
Bishop Odo, brother to William I,
the Bayeux Tapestry was worked by
English needlewomen, famed
throughout Europe for their *opus
anglicanum* embroidery, and
probably designed by an English
cleric living in Canterbury. David
Bernstein argues that, along with
the main text celebrating Norman
domination of England, there runs a
subtly irreverent subtext
challenging the official Norman view
of events.[23] Other embroiderers
have used their art for political ends
sometimes celebrating the status

quo and sometimes challenging it.[24]
As a prisoner in England, Mary
Queen of Scots embroidered
assiduously, sending some of her
work as offerings to Queen
Elizabeth. Other pieces, however,
were a way of commenting on her
own fate and even of
communicating with conspirators
who wished to assassinate
Elizabeth and place Mary on the
throne.[25] More recently, in 1985, a
group of US needlewomen encircled
the Pentagon with a fifteen-mile
long ribbon of embroidered fabric in
protest against nuclear war.[26]
During the Pinochet years in Chile,
working-class women embroidered
arpilleras—appliquéd pictures on
hessian backgrounds—recording
their daily lives and the suffering
caused through the
"disappearance" of loved ones
under an oppressive regime. As
these pieces became sought by
collectors throughout the world, the
Chillean government aimed to
confiscate and replace them with
"safe" embroideries produced and
traded under its own supervision.[27]

Embroiderers' Guild members
who volunteered their services for
work on the Parliament House
project may not have considered
they were engaging in political
activity, but placing an artwork in
the seat of government inevitably
gives it a political dimension. Kay
Lawrence's design is concerned with
"the land as a conditioner of
values" and with representing
landscape "as a means of
expressing fundamental ideas
about Australia" (PHE: 6). Lawrence
read very widely while developing
the design, being particularly
influenced by Geoffrey Bolton's
Spoils and Spoilers (1981).

I was surprised to discover, through my reading, the extent to which the landscape we take for granted as "natural and untouched" has been altered by human intervention—European agriculture and buildings, displacement of indigenous plants and animals, tree-cutting and so on. I eventually decided to use such changes to the land in my design as a metaphor for the development of European settlement in Australia. Then changes in the appearance of the land would symbolise the settlers' attempts to come to terms with their environment and to use the land properly (PHE: 7).

Her notes list the work's major topics: "The Land" with both Aboriginal and European responses to it; "Imposing European sensibility;" "Exploiting natural resources," and finally "Holding a balance between positive/negative effects" (*PHE*: 6).

Just as the Bayeux Tapestry commemorates a key event in English history, so Lawrence's design narrates how the process of European settlement in Australia affected the land. Consequently the embroidery presents a double narrative. One is the story, familiar from school textbooks, of pioneers establishing themselves in the country, facing adversity and building a nation. The other story recounts loss, with Aboriginal people's dispossession of their land, native species being crowded out by European farming practices, and the harmful introduction of exotic plants and animals. Celebration is, therefore, balanced and greatly modified by an elegiac tone. Representation of an Aboriginal presence by white artis[ts] and craftspeople is particularly sensitive. Well before a designer was appointed, ACT Guild membe[rs] undertook substantial research on motifs the design might incorporate. Although they considered using Aboriginal images, they decided against this "as it was highly probable that submissions would be made by th[e] Aboriginal Arts Board for works of Aboriginal Art to be displayed in t[he] New Parliament House."[28] Althou[gh] the building contains major indigenous artworks, the story of white settlement cannot be divorc[ed] from its effect on the original inhabitants. Lawrence's design negotiates problems of appropriation or speaking on beh[alf] of Aborigines through quotation o[f] verbal statements and visual images originally created by Aborigines themselves.

With the embroidery sixteen meters long and located in a galle[ry] only two meters wide, it becomes impossible to stand back and take in the entire work at a glance. Its positioning, one and a half meter[s] from the ground, allows visitors, including children, to view the wo[rk] at close quarters obliging them to read it closely as they walk along. Parliament House itself has been described as "a highly literary wor[k] set out like a great book that can b[e] read on many levels"[29] and Lawrence's design also contains a[] strong literary component. Like th[e] Latin commentary across the top o[f] the Bayeux Tapestry, a range of written texts appears in the Parliament House embroidery, mostly at the base of the design. Only one section, representing the ur seasons, has no words in it. ose affinity between language and xtiles has been acknowledged er centuries in such metaphors as pinning a yarn" or "following the read of a story," and detailed alogies have been proposed tween cloth making and mposing a narrative.[30] Margo ensing, a US textile artist and eorist, comments that artists' use language in many contemporary xtiles "exposes limits and ssibilities of language" and that rds are often "intended to teract with the object or surface to gister a new meaning based on is interplay."[31] In the Parliament House embroidery, text, cloth, and thread all complement one another.

The Narrative

The great length of the embroidery represents both the span of Australian history, from pre-European times until 1900, as well as the wide expanse of the continent from west to east. The design opens with an image of landscape resembling a headland facing left as if looking back into the past, and it closes with a similar landscape image facing right, looking out into the future. Time flows both ways beyond the boundaries of the cloth. The land is seen to underlay all life and human experience in Australia, enduring steadily despite changes imposed upon it. Lawrence avoids standard landscape clichés. There are no allusions to "the Grotesque," "the Weird," the dead heart, the red center or even the wide brown land. The initial landscape (Figure 1) image represents tranquil, undulating country in soft, muted greens, with here and there touches of russet, brown, and beige, while the concluding image contains similar contours and colors though with added touches of blue on the hills.

Figure 1
CT Embroiderers' Guild Members. First Landscape, detail from the panel, 2000 × 650 mm. "Aborginal Response to the Land." ewel wool on glenshee linen. 1988. Courtesy of the ACT Embroiderers' Guild.

Human figures, mostly derived from drawings, paintings, and early photographs, are also incorporated into the embroidery. Ivor Indyk comments that it is "one of the few art works in the building to contain specifically historical or social references—but it does so from the land's point of view."[32]

Like the Bayeux Tapestry, the overall design is organized in panels, each embroidered by members of a different State or Territory guild, with these subdivided vertically into smaller sections so that the general effect has been compared to a series of film stills. The opening panel, stitched by ACT embroiderers, represents a land infused with Aboriginal presence summed up in

writer Sam Woolagoodjah's words in the Worora language which translate as, "These places hold o[r] spirits, these Wunga places of the[r] Wandjinas."[33] Alongside the opening landscape is the close-u[p] image of an Aboriginal rock carvin[g] followed by a detail from *Possum Dreaming*, a contemporary Papun[a] dot painting, juxtaposed with an aerial photograph of Lake Eyre (Figure 3). Translating Lawrence's original ink, crayon, and gouache drawings into stitchery required great imagination, patience, and technical skill from all the embroiderers. A sense of this complexity is present in their account of embroidering the Aboriginal petroglyph (from Red Gorge in South Australia's Flinder[s]

Figure 2
ACT Embroiderers' Guild Members. First Landscape (detail). Courtesy of the ACT Embroiderers' Guild.

‚ure 3
‚T Embroiderers' Guild Members. Completed panel, "Aboriginal response to the land", 200 × 650 mm. Crewel wool and ‚ercerised cotton on glenshee linen. 1988. Courtesy ACT Embroiderers' Guild.

nges), which depicts an emu ‚otprint with circles and spots ‚gnifying emu and goanna ‚cks.[34]

The section was worked entirely ‚n wool, often two colours of ‚hread in the one needle. Some ‚of the watercolour and crayon ‚shadings were especially difficult ‚o achieve. Shades of blue-grey ‚anging to pink, apricot and ‚orange were worked in straight ‚stitches to give the background ‚the appearance of a rough, flaky ‚rock surface. Cretan stitch was ‚used to depict the embedded ‚emu claw (PHE: 23).

Some of the blue tonings in the petroglyph segment reappear in *Possum Dreaming* offset by a darker meandering movement which seems to flow into the adjacent image of Lake Eyre minimizing the distinction between them.

In Lawrence's design, curves and meanders are associated both with the land and Aboriginal perceptions of it. The next panel, worked by Queensland embroiderers, shows European attempts to contain and control this sinuosity with straight lines and a mapmaker's grid (Figure 4). Three maps, side by side, "show different Aboriginal and European interpretations of land settlement

and division" (*PHE*: 25). The first indicates distinctions between South Australian Aborigines based on tribal language groups at the time of European settlement. Those boundary lines show the arbitrariness of State boundaries (stitched in red) by reaching across them in a meandering pattern similar to the images of *Possum Dreaming* and Lake Eyre. An attempt is made to net everything in place with a fine grid. A clearly defined space separates this map from the next, a representation of Brisbane in 1844 by C. F. Gerler which offers a compromise between straight lines and curves. Streets, with their four-square houses are carefully ruled, but a river winds through the town with trees and bushes scattered round. A more forceful grid appears in the adjacent military map of Brisbane where space is ruled emphatically, not only with a criss-cross of streets, but through names imposed in block letters indicating royal authority and power—Queen, Elizabeth, Charlotte, William, George. The design here is stitched over a transparent overlay dyed to resemble Lawrence's original gouache sketch depicting "uneven terrain or perhaps a discoloured parchment map" (*PHE*: 27). The faint colors also echo tonings in the opening landscape, showing the land now dominated by schemas imposed by European culture.

Colonial authorities mapped and surveyed land to allocate or sell to settlers who farmed and built on it. Embroidered by Tasmanian guild members, the next panel, with images of pioneer houses and their builders, is about establishing home. First is a representation of John Glover's iconic painting (*c*. 1840) of his house and garden in Tasmania, now hanging in the South Australian Art Gallery (Figure 5). Glover paints a profusic of English flowers—roses, hollyhocks, broom, and foxgloves in garden beds which lead to a substantial stone house set again bush-covered hills with palm trees off to the right. Although Glover blends bush and garden harmoniously, the native plants appear exotic, while the English exotics communicate a sense of home. Lawrence simplifies his painting to a sketched outline, but her substitution of a largely monochromatic image for the golc reds, and pinks of Glover's garden caused some dismay.

It should be stated that when those of us in the Tasmanian group first saw the images we were to embroider we were deeply disappointed. It seemed almost all black and we wanted to use colour and to create prettier images (PHE: 28).

Lawrence herself is a tapestry weaver, not an embroiderer, and interpreting her design involved

Figure 4
Kay Lawrence, "European Response: Mapping the Land," original design (approx. 13 × 40 cm) for panel to be worked by Queensland Embroiderers' Guild Members. Pen and ink, pencil, gourache. 1984. Courtesy Kay Lawrence.

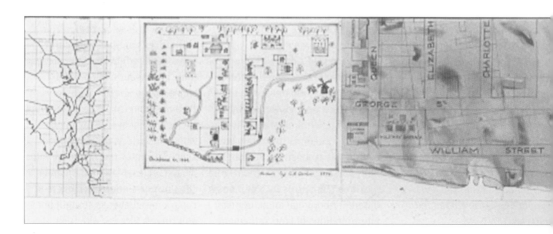

Figure 5

Tasmanian Embroiderers' Guild Members. "Glover's House," detail from panel, 2000 × 650mm, "The Dream and the Reality." Jewel wool on glenshee linen. 1988. Courtesy ACT Embroiderers' Guild.

considerable negotiation between herself, the embroiderers, and Anne Richards, national coordinator for the project. Color appears to have been a recurring issue. The work moves from color through a largely monochromatic area and back again to color, though its general use of color is muted and subdued. Compared to the massive tapestry, designed by painter Arthur Boyd, in the Hall below, which portrays the bush in brilliant golds and ochers with flashes of vibrant blue sky set off by pale tree trunks and white cockatoo plumage, the Parliament House embroidery appears austere and restrained. Embroidery is

capable of both brilliant color effects and sumptuous textures, so many of the Parliament House embroiderers may have yearned to display the more lavish aspects of their art, particularly since gardens, in all their variety of color and texture, have long been a major embroidery motif. "Never before had the embroiderers worked charcoal foliage and beige-toned roses!" (*PHE*: 28). But, as Anne Richards points out, they rose to the challenge of creating black and sepia hollyhocks "by blending a variety of matt and shiny threads in a rich tonal surface. This contrast of yarns creates an exciting new

dimension and quality that the artist had not anticipated."[35]

Lawrence's choice of style and color emphasizes the abstract idea behind Glover's painting. Like lines on maps, house and garden becomes yet another schema imposed on the landscape, and one still prominent in contemporary Australian consciousness. The remainder of the panel shows how arduously that ideal was realized. A nineteenth-century settler's cottage is placed next to the Glover image (Figure 6). Here there is no sense of harmony with the surrounding bush, much of which lies as a scattering of felled tree-trunks, while a couple of remaining trees form strong verticals across the facade of the house. Embroidered below is an extract from Mary Thomas's letter of 7 April, 1859 revealing how she yearns to grow a familiar English plant.

> *Likewise I want a root of rhubarb . . . You will think me very silly but I cannot help it, for I have such a desire for something English that nothing else gives me any pleasure (PHE: 29).*

Alongside are portraits of pioneers reproduced from early photographs. One shows a man in work clothes standing before a portable shed and inscribed "William Allen. Workshop W.A." The other captures a man and woman apparently levering a heavy log off the ground. The embroiderers were happier with monochrome portrayals of early settlers, feeling that the limited color "expressed the bleak conditions of the time" (*PHE*: 13–14).

Debate between the embroiderers and Lawrence involved not only artistic and technical considerations, but also the ideas expressed in the design. Not all were happy with Lawrence's ideological position. "A few were offended by references to the exploitation of the land by the early settlers," but through discussing and working on the design many of their objections were overcome (*PHE*: 30). The South Australian embroiderers who worked on the next panel showing the four seasons were disappointed their

Figure 6
Tasmanian Embroiderers' Guild Members. "Settler's Cottage," detail from panel "The Dream and the Reality. Crewel wool on glenshee linen. 1988. Courtesy ACT Embroiderers' Guild.

ntribution was to stitch cleared
ls and bushfire: "However, when
e understood the concept better
d realised that the images were
oresentative of the impact of
ropean settlement on the country
a whole, we felt happier" (*PHE*:
). The succession of the four
asons has long been a standard
abroidery motif,[36] but Lawrence
esents an antipodean version. Her
ion of autumn is no "Season of
sts and mellow fruitfulness" but a
eached, gray landscape with
eaks of gold running through it.
es ruled on the map by European
ttlement are represented by fence
osts marching across undulating
ddocks, with blackened stumps
d tree trunks scattered round.
insparent dyed overlays help
rtray winter and spring as gentle
asons, the former stitched in pale
ld and green, while the latter
esents a deeper green with some
ue and gray intermingled. A
riped crescent shape, mainly
ite and red, curls over a hill
the middle distance. "Kay
nningly left it to each individual
decide whether [it] was a
nbow or a road leading
mewhere" (*PHE*: 31). Road and
nbow both indicate promise, but
ring leads into a summer
idscape ravaged by bushfire
d, once again, there is a stark
age of the land barred with rows
blackened tree trunks. Europeans
ve taken possession of
rmidable terrain.

Nevertheless they reaped rich
wards. The subsequent panel,
orked by New South Wales
abroiderers, shows a land fertile
d abundant both before and after
ite colonization, with gain and
ss inextricably entwined. A

quotation from Geoffrey Bolton's
Spoils and Spoilers runs beneath
the images binding them together.
"Sheep and rabbits have ensured
that we shall never again see the
waving plains of Mitchell grass or
the rich and diverse native herbiage
the Aborigines knew and worked"
(*PHE*: 32). The first image is a field of
Mitchell grass, followed by another
showing stalks of ripe wheat
swaying in the wind. Worked in
negative form, the Mitchell grass
appears ghostly, defined by spaces
left between rows of dark stitching,
which depict shading and shadows.
The wheat, however, gleams rich
and sensuous against the linen
background.

Subtle tonings of predominantly
warm golds, creams, fawns and
occasional touches of apricot,
pink and mauve-grey created the
variety of colour in the
wheatheads (PHE: 35).

Lawrence invests her image with the
potent array of associations grain
carries in European culture—fertility,
fulfillment, and the joy of harvest
home.

A pastoral scene follows with
sheep grazing on a golden hillside
shading into distant mauve.
Pastoral scenes are also highly
charged in European literary and
artistic tradition, representing
innocence, peace, and a possible
withdrawal from worldly cares and
responsibilities. The grain and
sheep are not merely sources of
material wealth representing
Australia's major agricultural
products, but indicators of the rich
cultural heritage which
accompanied European settlement.
Such riches, however, prove costly.

In a corner to the right of the
pastoral scene is the image of a
potoroo, the precariousness of its
present existence indicated by a
diagonal cross stitched over it, as if
canceling the animal out (Figure 7).

The cross through the potoroo
caused much controversy. A
compromise was reached by
breaking one of the arms of the
cross to indicate that it is an
endangered, not an extinct
species (PHE: 35).

Whereas the Mitchell grass appears
insubstantial when contrasted
against the wheat, the potoroo
stands out much more sharply than
the sheep which have been
embroidered largely in outline so
the landscape seems to shine
through them. Sheep are now so
much part of the land that they
merge with it, whereas the
potoroo's sharply defined, finely
detailed image appears more like a
zoological illustration than the
representation of a living animal.

The land's fertility is both a
blessing and a burden. Native
species are extinguished while,
without appropriate environmental
controls, introduced ones have
multiplied alarmingly. Such pests
figure in the next panel, stitched by
Northern Territory embroiderers who
found the subject disconcerting:
"Initially our members were not
happy about portraying these
scourges" (*PHE*: 36). Two plant
images appear, one above the
other. Outlined in black, they
resemble botanical drawings with
scientific names printed beneath.
On top is Patterson's curse (also
known as salvation Jane) with an
example of prickly pear cactus

below. The images emphasize each plant's fecundity and the prickly pear spines add a touch of menace. Their presence relates to the endangered potoroo in the previous panel which also resembles a scientific drawing with its name lettered underneath. Extinction and excess proliferation go hand in hand. Humor pervades the rest of the panel which recreates artist Sam Burns's painting "Hungry Rabbits Thackaringa 1890 Drought" (Figure 8). Two women and a couple of children stand outside neighboring houses which echo both the Glover house and the settler cottage seen earlier. Instead of flowers, however, or even tree stumps, houses and people are surrounded by a multitude of rabbits. Each child holds one and the women empty scraps from saucepans to feed them. Cute animals make cuddly domestic pets whilst also ravaging the landscape, represented here by the pale green/ gold overlay on which the embroidery has been worked.

The next panel, embroidered by Victorian guild members, represents a town, its people and their activities. A row of pioneer implements appears on the left, while on the far right are a group of those who may have made or used them, with the town spread out between. A mattock, wheel, pitchfork and three-legged stool are all embroidered one above the other in threads a few shades darker than the linen ground. Read downwards the "shapes of the implements approximate the letters which spell 'town'" (*PHE*: 38). Images, derived mostly from old daguerrotypes of nineteenth-century working people suggest the bustle of a country town. A shopkeeper stands outside her store and a group of plumbers pose before a facade emblazoned with the word "contractors." Embroidered below them is a statement from the *Australian Financial Gazette* of 1890 indicating Australian preoccupation with home ownership: ". . . the first, the paramount duty of a working man

acquire a home." To the right is a
iner shoveling ore and above him
e figure of a woman from an S. T.
ll drawing who works a gold
adle with one hand while holding
er baby with the other.

By comparison, the town in the
nter appears insubstantial. It is
e abstraction of a town, another
hema imposed on the landscape.
ouses in shades of grey and white
e appliquéd onto a dull gold
llside and some are merely
ketched in with fine black lines
hich also mark out a grid of
reets. Scattered marks on the
ound suggest building detritus

lying around. This image is closed
off to the right by a thin, vertical
strip of patchwork, itself an artefact,
which corresponds to the row of
implements on the other side, and a
design of patchwork diamonds lies
across the base of the landscape.
Despite its sharp angles, the
diamond pattern appears to form
another land contour. The plain
patches are mostly in shades of
green, gold, russet, and brown—
colors assigned to the land
throughout the embroidery—while
the other pieces are mainly
patterned with flowers and leaves
suggesting the gardens settlers

grew. This patchwork section forms
a self-reflexive comment on the
entire work, drawing attention to
how the embroidery seeks to
recreate the land through cloth and
thread. Below is a poignant
comment from a Taunguiang
tribesman quoted in Henry
Reynolds' *The Other Side of the
Frontier*: "Black fellow by and by all
gone, plenty shoot 'em white fellow
. . . long time plenty, plenty" (*PHE*:
38). Just as European-style
agriculture and introduced pests
have jeopardized native plants and
animals, sometimes to the point of
extinction, so European eagerness

gure 8
orthern Territory Embroiderers' Guild Members. "Hungry Rabbits Thackaringa 1890 Drought," detail from panel 1218 × 650
m, "Changes to the Land; Introduced Pests." Crewel wool and applique on glenshee linen. 1988. Courtesy of the ACT
nbroiderers' Guild.

for land, and the imposition of an alien culture, have profoundly damaged Aborigines and their way of life. The plenty acquired with such hard work by white settlers involved the killing of "plenty, plenty" indigenous people. Gain is once again shadowed by loss.

Houses, agriculture and urbanization lead to industrial activity featured in the final panel worked by Western Australian embroiderers (Figure 9). Alongside images of miners in the previous panel is a mining town, its houses clustered near the horizon and surrounded by mounds of coal, dominated by a tall chimney and the mine poppet-head. An expanse of faded, unloved landscape, stitched in beige, light grey and pale gold, fills the foreground. Black markings suggest tree trunks stripped of foliage and piles of wood or rubble. Fitted beside this scene so exactly that both share the same horizon, is a soft green landscape with trees and shrubs, a representation of the land's ability to endure and retain its essential character. Inscribed beneath both images, binding them

together, are lines from the conclusion of Judith Wright's poem "Falls Country."[37]

> There is
> there was
> a country
> that spoke in the language of
> leaves.

The lettering, embroidered in white thread, "appears as a whisper" against the pale mining scene "but as the words stand out against the landscape the strength of this affirmation of the land seems to increase in volume and power" (*PHE*: 43). Wright's poem claims th those who live attuned to the land can learn to understand and speak its language of leaves, urging the reader, "latecomer to my country/ sharer in what I know/eater of wild manna" to listen to it, although the juxtaposition of present and past tenses—"There is/there was" implies the language is in danger o disappearing.

Although this final image of the land resembles the pre-European vision shown earlier in the

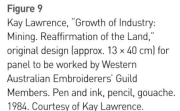

Figure 9
Kay Lawrence, "Growth of Industry: Mining. Reaffirmation of the Land," original design (approx. 13 × 40 cm) for panel to be worked by Western Australian Embroiderers' Guild Members. Pen and ink, pencil, gouache. 1984. Courtesy of Kay Lawrence.

broidery, Lawrence cuts right
ross it with a pale vertical line
parating off its outer edge. While
e land endures and parts of it still
ok much as they always have, it
s been irretrievably marked by
o centuries of white habitation.
t the edge of land beyond this
viding line may also signify a
ssible new beginning with a new
t of responses to where we live.
e white flash of Halley's comet
ove the horizon points forward.
e comet was included partly as an
usion to its appearance in the
yeux Tapestry and partly because
appeared in 1986 when the
broidery was being stitched, but
also represents the natural world
th its recurring cycles and its
wer of endurance.

nclusion

th five hundred embroiderers
ntributing, the Parliament House
broidery is both a remarkable
gistical achievement and an
pressive co-operative effort, "a
ork of many hands," as the book
scribing the work is sub-titled.
oosing appropriate threads,
lors, and stitches to recreate the
iginal design as accurately
ssible as well as maintaining
nservation values to ensure the
broidery's long-term survival,
oved very exacting. Many of the
broiderers, however, have
mmented on the strong sense of
mradeship which developed
tween them and the pleasure of
tching and discussing their work
gether. They drew, with immense
rtuosity, on textile skills women
ve practiced over centuries and,
though a number may have felt
ey were asked to adapt their art in

outlandish ways, Lawrence has
incorporated many traditional
embroidery motifs. Generations of
little girls have stitched their
samplers with a variety of
quotations. Images of house and
garden have been popular with
embroiderers since Elizabethan
times and representations of new
and unusual plant species have
frequently been incorporated in
their work.[38] Pastoral scenes
showing bountiful fields and flocks
of sheep were popular among
eighteenth-century embroiderers.[39]
Embroidery is a particularly
appropriate medium to represent
fertility, for this was originally one of
its principal functions and symbols
of fruitfulness still form part of the
embroiderer's repertoire, though
their original significance is long
forgotten.[40]

Lawrence subverts many of
these motifs by negating their
conventional "prettiness" to make
observers think more carefully
about the images set before them.
The work's strong literary
associations assist in this with its
quotation of authors such as Judith
Wright providing links and contrasts
to the prose passages under glass
at the entry to the Great Hall.
Embroidery is readily dismissed as
mere feminine embellishment, but
in the Parliament House embroidery
it expresses ideas of national
importance and raises some
difficult questions. What does it
mean to call Australia home? Who is
at home there and who is not? What
has it cost to establish this
homeland and who has paid the
greatest price? The land is portrayed
with a mixture of sorrow and tender
affection, but the long span of the
embroidery concludes with hopes

that if Australians learn to love and
cherish it more deeply, they will
ultimately feel more completely at
home in it. In Lawrence's own
words:

*Mistakes made in the
development of the land are not
glossed over but the final
landscape, reminiscent of the
first gentle image, suggests a
growing awareness of our
responsibility and an
acknowledgment of our
indebtedness to the land we
have made ours (PHE: 11).*

In 2003, it is possible to see how
presciently the Parliament House
Embroidery foreshadowed current
debates over the uneasy position
Europeans occupy in the Australian
landscape. A sense of loss and
anxiety, together with the
interrogation of myths of pioneer
"heroism," are all expressed
through the work's composition,
selection of images, tones, and
complexity of stitching. When in
1998 members of the ACT
Embroiderers' Guild put together a
small traveling exhibition of
experimental samplers, fabrics, and
threads celebrating the tenth
anniversary of the work's
completion, their accompanying
flyer asserts it is "Regarded by many
as the most powerful political
statement in the Parliament House
Art Collection." With time, that
statement has only increased in
power.

Acknowledgments
I have accrued many debts of
gratitude in writing this paper. Kay
Lawrence, Dorothy Hyslop, Gabrielle
Hyslop, and members of the ACT

Embroiders' Guild gave generously of their time to talk to me and provided access to valuable archival material. Colleagues Paul Sharrad, Anne Collett and Diana Wood Conroy offered helpful comment and Lycia Trouton provided invaluable research assistance.

The illustrations accompanying this paper are from Kay Lawrence, *Parliament House Embroidery* (1984–88). Executed and presented by the embroiderers' Guild of Australia. Parliament House Gift Collection, Canberra. Courtesy of Parliament House Art Collection, Joint House Department, Canberra ACT.

Notes

1. Although the Guilds are open to both black and white members, a marked cultural gap between the races in rural areas has resulted in very few Aboriginal members.
2. Kay Lawrence (b. 1947) is currently head of the South Australian School of Art in the University of South Australia. One of Australia's foremost textile artists and teachers, she studied weaving under Archie Brennan at the Edinburgh College of Art. She has produced numerous tapestries, many inspired by Australian landscape. A number of her works, like the Parliament House Embroidery and the Women's Suffrage Centenary Tapestries hanging in the Legislative Chamber of the South Australian Parliament, have been community projects.
3. Charles T. Goodsell, The Social Meaning of Civic Space. Studying Political Authority Through Architecture (Lawrence KA: Kansas University Press, 1988), p. 8.
4. For detailed discussion see David Rosand, Myths of Venice The Figuration of a State (Chapel Hill NC and London: University of North Carolina Press), 2001.
5. Expressing Australia, Art in Parliament House (Canberra: Joint House Department of Parliament House, 1993), p. 9.
6. Ivor Indyk, "The Semiotics of the New Parliament House," in Parliament House Canberra: A Building for the Nation, ed. H. Beck (Sydney: Collins, 1988), p. 44.
7. Livio Dobrez, "'Late' and 'Post' Nationalisms: Reappropriation and Problematization in Recent Australian Cultural Discourse," in Australian Nationalism Reconsidered. Maintaining a Monocultural Tradition in a Multicultural Society, ed. Adi Wimmer (Tübingen: Stauffenberg Verlag, 1999), p.
8. Philip Drew, The Coast Dwellers A Radical Reappraisal of Australian Identity (Ringwood: Penguin Australia, 1994), pp. 61–7.
9. Simon Schama, Landscape and Memory (London: Harper Collins, 1995), p. 15.
10. Indyk, *Parliament House Canberra*, p. 45.
11. *Ibid*, p. 46.
12. Conservative politicians and historians have criticised histories emphasizing white settlers' cruelty and oppression of Aborigines as a "black armband" view of history while writers minimizing this are

described as wearing "white blindfolds."

3. Schama, *Landscape and Memory*, p. 61.

4. *Expressing Australia*, p. 9.

5. Jennifer Taylor, "Parliament House Symbolism," in *Progressive Architecture* August 1988, 101.

6. Douglas Smith, *Interpreting the Art and Design of Parliament House* (Canberra: Royal Australian Institute of Architects, 1989), p. 12.

7. J. C. Beaglehole, ed., *The Journals of Captain James Cook on His Voyage of Discovery*. Vol. 1. *The Voyage of The Endeavour 1768–1771* (Cambridge: Cambridge University Press, 1955), p. 399.

8. Marcus Clarke, "Preface to Gordon's Poems," in *The Writer in Australia 1856–1964*, ed. John Barnes (Melbourne: Oxford University Press, 1969), p. 36.

9. Tom Griffiths, "A Haunted Country?" in *Land and Identity*, ed. Jennifer McDonnell and Michael Dewes (Adelaide: Association for the Study of Australian Literature, 1998), pp. 1–2.

10. The Parliament House Embroidery Committee, *The Parliament House Embroidery. A Work of Many Hands* (Canberra: AGPS Press, 1994), p. 6. Referred to hereafter as *PHE*. Further references given in the text.

11. Rozsika Parker explores this idea in *The Subversive Stitch. Embroidery and the Making of the Feminine* (London: Virago, 1984). See particularly pp. 1–16.

22. Dorothy Hyslop, "Narrative Embroidery," in *Textile Fibre Forum* 6(18). 1987, 10.

23. David J. Bernstein, *The Mystery of the Bayeux Tapestry* (London: Weidenfeld & Nicolson, 1986).

24. For some Australian examples see Jennifer Isaacs, *The Gentle Arts. 200 Years of Australian Women's domestic and Decorative Arts* (Sydney: Ure Smith, 1987), pp. 182–95.

25. Margaret Swain, *The Needlework of Mary Queen of Scots* (New York: Van Nostrand Reinhold, 1973). See particularly pp. 75–8.

26. Linda Pershing, "Peace Work out of Piecework: Feminist Needlework Metaphors and The Ribbon around the Pentagon," in *Feminist Theory and the Study of Folklore*, ed. Susan Tower Hillis, Linda Pershing and M. Jane Young (Urbana and Chicago IL: Univeristy of Illinois Press, 1993), pp. 327–57.

27. Marjorie Agosín, *Tapestries of Hope, Threads of Love*, trans. Celeste Kostopulous-Cooperman, (Albuquerque NM: University of New Mexico Press, 1996), p. xii.

28. Barb Haynes, "New Parliament House Embroidery," Aboriginal Designs, 15.9.81, Australian National Library, Ms. no. 8369, Box 9.

29. Taylor, *Progressive Architecture*, p. 100.

30. See Susan M. Pearce, "Foreword: Words and Things," *Experiencing Material Culture in the Western World* (London and Washington DC: Leicester University Press, 1997), p. 3.

31. Margo Mensing. 1997. "Dissolving Language. What the Unreadable Tells Us About Words," *Fibrearts*, 23(4), 45.

32. Indyk, *Parliament House Canberra*, p. 45.

33. "The Wandjinas are spirit people of the Kimberly region of north-western Australia. The Wandjinas are believed to have come from the sea and sky originally, and the rocks, springs and other features of the landscape now hold their spirits" *PHE*: 22.

34. Another textile version of the same petroglyph appears in Kay Lawrence's tapestry *Red Gorge, two views* which hangs in the dining room in the Prime Minister's suite in Parliament House.

35. Anne Richards. 1987. "Parliament House Embroidery," *Textile Fibre Forum*, 6(1), 8.

36. Parker, *The Subversive Stitch*, p. 94.

37. Judith Wright (1915–2000) is one of Australia's foremost twentieth-century poets and particularly noted for her vision of its landscape. "Falls Country" appears in her 1973 collection *Alive: Poems 1971–72* (Sydney: Angus and Robertson, 1973), pp. 36–7.

38. Parker, *The Subversive Stitch*, p. 72.

39. *Ibid.*, p. 116.

40. Sheila Paine, *Embroidered Textiles* (London: Thames and Hudson, 1995), pp. 780–1. See also Parker, *The Subversive Stitch*, p. 94.

Exhibition Review

Unfolding Territories. Faculty of Creative Arts,
University of Wollongong, Australia.

Exhibition Review
Unfolding Territories. Faculty of Creative Arts, University of Wollongong, Australia.

*Both textile and text form the fabric of a postcolonial transformative
dynamic that weaves its way/beats a path to and fro towards complex
cultural self-determinations.*

Paul Sharrad, *"Trading and Trade-offs," New Literatures Review,
(un)fabricating empire, No. 36, Winter 2000)*[1]

Unfolding Territories was the title of a textiles exhibition held in conjunction with the international conference *Fabric(ation)s of the Postcolonial* at the University of Wollongong in Australia in December 2002.[2] This exhibit came at the end of a year that celebrated the art of textiles globally and, particularly, on the pan-Pacific Rim. Key forums and exhibitions included *Intertwine* at the Adelaide Festival, South Australia, *Textile Tides—Convergence 2002*, in Vancouver, Canada, *Through the Eye of a Needle* at the Vancouver Museum, Vancouver, Canada, and *Splendorform: Elizabeth Jameson* at the Henry Art Gallery, University of Washington, Seattle.[3]

The unraveling stories of shifts in territorial political boundaries and the results of shifting identities which play out in our postcolonial period may best be told by exploring the layers of meaning and discoveries held in the folds of contemporary fabric arts. The artists showcased in *Unfolding Territories* have developed artwork out of investigations into such new cultural parameters and recent critical dialogue, influenced by theorists such as Sarat Maharaj, Gayatri Chakrovorty Spivak, and Nicholas Thomas. As Janis Jefferies stated in the conference keynote address, "cloth is a powerful metaphor for cultural translation . . . a moment's reflection brings to mind any number of feelings and experiences in which cloth, thread, and fabric are embedded in the metaphoric use of textiles to illuminate social and political relations. Within this context my

REVIEWED BY
LYCIA DANIELLE TROUTON

Textile, Volume 1, Issue 2, pp. 194–199
Reprints available directly from the Publishers.
Photocopying permitted by licence only.
© 2003 Berg. Printed in the United Kingdom.

own practice—exploring the intersection between the personal and the political—takes textiles and cloth as a starting point."

The relationship of textiles to the history of colonizing territories and developing sociocultural definitions of landscape, particularly in Australia, can be seen in the work of exhibitors Beth Hatton, Kay Lawrence, Liz Jeneid, Yvonne Koolmatrie, and Diana Wood Conroy, and in materials ranging from embroidery to tapestry, printed fabrics or cast paper. In her catalog essay, Diana Wood Conroy reiterated the often-stated claim of Australian art communities that:

It is a commonplace in Australian art history that our culture is haunted by the dispossession

Figure 1
Yvonne Koolmatrie, *Burial Basket*, 2002, rush basketry.

and violence done to Aborigines and this anxiety has given rise to melancholia in non-Aboriginal arts practice.[4]

Koolmatrie, a Ngarrindjeri weaver, displayed a haunting coffin basket from the burial tradition so important to her culture. Contemporary Tiwi funerary armbands and feathered ornaments from the family of Josette Orsto, which mark relationships to deceased members of her tribe, were displayed alongside a length of printed fabric representing body adornment by Tiwi artist, Jean Baptiste Apuatimi. Penny Harris, an

Australian sculptor, displayed a pair of old shoes cast in bronze, with a delicately textured patina, set on a wire bed frame. The installation evoked a ghostly mood and, as her title suggests, a "Waiting." Sue Blanchfield's work beseeched viewers to question consumer tastes considered fashionably exotic by awkwardly juxtaposing an early colonial image as the pattern for a typical Yirrkala, a Northern Territory community-store simple shift dress, recontextualized in transparent silk organza. The image Blanchfield chose for the printed repeat is a rescaled version of a famous historical moment in Australia,

recorded by the well-known Port Jackson painter in 1798, which records first contact.[5] The artist has chosen to comment upon specific elements of this painting and to play with our sensibilities by applying the revised version of the narrative as images on the kind of dress still worn by the indigenous women in northern parts of Australia. The image Blanchfield repeats is of the lone Aboriginal, Barrangaroo, wife of Bennelong, in her canoe, and a rowboat containing Governor Phillip and his eight armed men, thus illustrating the dramatic inequality of indigenous/settler relations[6] which

Figure 2
Ruth Hadlow, *Aeroplane Parts* (detail), 1998, installation of seventy pieces of cloth pinned to the wall

still continues today, albeit perhaps in other forms. Kelly Thompson, from New Zealand, works with both organic and mapping imagery, and is interested in the interchange between eighteenth century Maori and European explorers. Her thoughtful monochromatic works are mediated by the interface of using digital Jacquard loom technology. Ruth Hadlow, another Australian artist presently living in West Timor, compares the Ngarrindjeri coiling stitch of indigenous artist, Janet Watson, in the 1920s, to her own artistry of buttonhole and blanket-stitch embroidery to construct the image of a plane developed from over seventy small fabric samples. Hadlow has, in a sense, collaborated in Watson's earlier vision and comments on "how planes used to be fragile things . . . vulnerable and so hopeful . . ."[7] This pristine artwork installation, made in 1998, with its sensuous off-white sheen, is a particularly eerie image given the twisted weapon of destruction we now associate with aeroplanes in the wake of the events of 9/11.

Other artists in the exhibit investigated their experience and identities as migrants, such as Valerie Kirk from Scotland, my own background in Northern Ireland, while a shawl patterned with complex symbolism from Kalate Nadesi, North Iran, was brought to the exhibition by conference keynote presenter Jasleen Dhamija from New Delhi.[8]

The postcolonial world has inherited a situation of continual dislocation, and artists will most likely continue to grapple with questions such as those posed in this exhibition. In Australia, the locus of much textile arts practice involves a complex connection to the land and both on-going and historical relations with indigenous peoples. Through the creation of hybrid cultural objects and a reexamination of the position of historical textile artifacts, artists will develop personal and political narratives that will unfold to critique culture as we know it. The lessons that curator Diana Wood Conroy offered conference attendees as a result of her immersion in the very different traditions of the Aboriginal Tiwi culture (from Bathurst and Melville Islands, Northern Australia), and as an archaeologist in the Greco-Roman traditions of the Mediterranean, perhaps illustrate most poignantly how contemporary artists deal with a type of "double grounding"[9] and demonstrate that the textiles arena offers such artists a powerful medium for further investigations of the body, trade patterns, storytelling, and identity.

Notes

1. Published by the Centre for Research in Textual and Cultural Studies, University of Wollongong; the School of Humanities, University of Tasmania, Launceston; the Department of English, University of New South Wales; and the Faculty of Arts/School of Humanities & Social Sciences, Charles Sturt University.

2. Funded in part by an Australian Research Council Discovery Grant garnered by four key researchers in the disciplines of English Studies and Creative Arts at the University of Wollongong.

In 2003, "new artistic and theoretical potentialities that have emerged as a result of blurring boundaries between art, fashion and textiles," forming hybrid practices, will be explored at another conference, entitled *The Space Between* at Curtin University of Technology in Perth, Australia.

See, for example, Griffiths, Tom. *Hunters and Collectors: The Antiquarian Imagination in Australia*, p. 3. Cambridge: Cambridge University Press, 1996 and McLean, Ian. "Under Saturn: Melancholy and the Colonial Imagination," in Thomas, Nicholas and Losche, Diane (eds), *Double Vision: Art Histories and Colonial Histories in the Pacific*, pp. 131–6. Cambridge: Cambridge University Press, 1999.

This painting is by an unidentified painter called the Port Jackson painter who produced a large body of work in Australia at the time of first contact, *c.* 1790s (see Emmett, Peter. *Fleeting Encounters: Pictures and Chronicles of the First Fleet*. Glebe, NSW: Historic Houses Trust of New South Wales, 1995. This exhibition enabled Australians to view paintings many had not seen before from the collections held in British museums. In the original painting Governor Phillip, two officers, and eight armed men are in the background, bearing down upon the Aboriginals in fragile canoes, including Barrangaroo by herself (which is one of the few illustrations of a woman in a canoe, although Aboriginal women in Botany Bay and Port Jackson were fisherwomen). The artist has produced a feminist retelling of these elements to illustrate the overlooked but often sophisticated understanding of the female Aboriginals such as Barrangaroo, who tried to negotiate traditional kinship relations into the new settler system, and is now infamous for requesting to give birth in Government House in a symbolic act of establishing just such a relationship. The request was refused and is considered a crucial lost moment, especially by feminists, in the history of settler/indigenous relations in Australia.

6. In a conversation with this reviewer, in January 2003, Blanchfield stated that such dresses might be derived from the mission shifts of earlier this century, yet are still considered a standard and are sold today in shops in isolated communities at the top end of the Northern Territory, Australia. These simple dresses are typically imported, and may be the only outfit available for purchase by Aboriginal women. The artist hand-unpicked this shift, which she bought in Yirrkala in 2001, to make an exact replica copy. Blanchfield states that the transparency of her new art object relates to "seeing through the hypocrisy of how we still treat Aboriginals in this country."

7. Artists' statements, *Many Voices*, 13th Tamworth Fibre Textile Biennial catalogue, curator: Gill McCracken, p. 10. Sydney: SOS Printing, 1998.

8. Jasleen Dhamija said of the piece that it was "a poignant expression of the lives of Afghani women. The instruments of war, the burning houses and the air-field depicted on it reflect the environment in which it was created. More conventional motifs acquire a totally different significance. Multiple squares created along with stylized houses indicate the walls of the gutted homes. A yellow flower emerging out of a gun is a blast. Yet in the midst of this destruction there is hope, which is expressed by the creation of this tree of life budding with green leaves."

9. From Diana Wood Conroy's presentation paper entitled "The Knotted Self: Reflections on Postcolonial Textiles in Australia," delivered at the University of Wollongong conference, 28 November 2002.

Book Review

Anni Albers and Ancient American Textiles: From Bauhaus to Black Mountain
Virginia Gardner Troy

Book Review

Anni Albers and Ancient American Textiles: From Bauhaus to Black Mountain by **Virginia Gardner Troy (Ashgate Publishing, 2002)**

Anni Albers (1899–1994) can now safely be declared to be a "William Morris" of twentieth-century textiles, in that no other designer of her century has been accorded the equivalent combination of acclaim in her own lifetime and reassessment after her death. This volume is the third since 1999 to provide new insights into her work: the others are *Anni Albers: Selected Writings on Design* (Middletown, CT: Wesleyan University Press, 2001) with an insightful introduction by its editor, Brenda Danilowitz; and *Anni Albers* (New York: Abrams, 1999), which contains a series of essays including a perceptive biography by its principal editor, Nicholas Fox Weber—who is also the Executive Director of the Josef and Anni Albers Foundation—and "Thread as Text: The Woven Work of Anni Albers," by Troy herself. Aspects of the latter essay appear in the book under review, although readers familiar with Albers's scholarship will find much that is new.

Of particular interest are the first two chapters, which are allocated some one-quarter of the entire text and provide a pertinent summary of the impact of non-European material culture on many artists and writers in the first decades of the twentieth century, followed by a more detailed examination of the role of Andean textiles in German primitivist discourse and ethnographic scholarship from 1880–1930. The subjects covered have relevance beyond the confines of textiles *per se*: German applied arts and education reform, cultural theorists, curatorial practices and the contribution of what were then called "primitive" textiles to Expressionist artists including Kandinsky and Klee. For museologists, the discussion of German dominance of Peruvian archaeological digs is a welcome addition to existing literature, since it contextualizes the impact of Andean collections, with the largest being that of the Berlin Museum für Völkerkunde, with some 45,000 objects. The d'Harcourt publications on Peruvian textiles are also set in perspective; this small but significant detail is critical since most English-speaking audiences know *The Textiles of Ancient Peru and their Techniques*, a 1962 revision (and 1987 reprint) of the volume first published in Paris in 1934.

Textile, Volume 1, Issue 2, pp. 200–203
Reprints available directly from the Publishers.
Photocopying permitted by licence only.
© 2003 Berg. Printed in the United Kingdom.

EVIEWED BY MARY SCHOESER

Instead, German scholarship of 1880–23 is highlighted, setting the stage for the third and fourth chapters. In these the "Expressionist" years of the Bauhaus Weimar (1919–23) and Albers's years at the Bauhaus Dessau (1923–32) are examined in relation to Andean textiles and both the Weaving Workshop and Bauhaus pedagogy, particularly with regard to the concept of universalism. Troy gives a carefully judged assessment of the influence of "primitive" and folk art on Bauhaus weavers, arguing that when later denied by Gunta Stölzl, this reflected a desire to set the Bauhaus apart from the "racist beliefs prevalent in Germany from the twenties through the Nazi period which embraced northern European folk traditions as examples of pure Germanic folk expression."

The final three chapters cover the years during which Albers taught at Black Mountain College in North Carolina (1933–49) and her career as a weaver until she gave up her loom in 1966. The development of Albers's own teaching strategies and personal aesthetic are positioned as expressions of her prior regard for Andean textiles as well as her growing first-hand acquaintance with them. The whereabouts of examples she collected are also charted. However, this section is less convincing, as it becomes increasingly focused on Albers's artistic output and influence. It ignores a substantial body of knowledge to state without qualification that her utilitarian and abstract designs for industry (few of which were produced until the 1940s) inspired "artist-designers

. . . not to think of textiles in terms of figurative motifs or surface designs but to work with the appropriate materials and structure." One can also debate whether or not her pictorial weavings of the 1950s and 1960s "continue to serve as a standard against which many artists approach their work."

There are throughout questions to be raised regarding the author's isolation of Bauhaus and Albers textiles from those produced elsewhere. For example, while the chequerboard layout of Bauhaus textiles certainly appears similar to those on Andean examples, what more immediately springs to mind is the use of the same motif among artists associated with the Weiner Wërkstatte, the single most prolific and influential known source of *avant-garde* textiles between 1913 and 1932. Albers's interest in multilayered weaves, gauzes and, to some extent, mirrored repeats, could equally have arisen from long existing German weaving traditions in the absence of any given evidence, her "discovery" of pre-painting warps may not have derived from Andean scaffold weaving (an entirely different concept), but from exactly parallel techniques applied in Europe on both craft and industrial scale since the nineteenth century. The lyrical text surrounding the description of Albers's diploma cloth of 1929—"a clever, and totally modern, version of the double weave"—emphasizes the cleverness over the variation on a theme, and in doing so suggests that acoustic wall-coverings, wear-testing, and the hand-weaving of prototypes for powered production were all equally novel. Most portantly, placing Albers as lead-omoter of Andean textiles does t acknowledge the ground broken initiatives taken from World War I til the late 1920s in the United ates and promoting non-European xtiles as models for modern oduction. That the majority of the sulting textiles were printed (as re many of the Wërkstatte signs) does not justify exempting eir influence from what is otherwise an excellent contextualization of the evolution of an individual weaver's pedagogy, especially since these initiatives, too, were based on the use of museum collections of ethnographic material. Finally, while the book itself is meticulous in its presentation of text and notes, the illustrations appear to have been overlooked by the designer. To no benefit all but four black-and-white illustrations are placed on picture-only pages with the result that several are far too small. They are not numbered in sequence, because there is no different sequence for the color plates, set apart in two sections. The result is that the reader must search backward and forward: to consult 3.9–3.13, for example, one must consult pages 65, 55, 54, 54, and 65 again. Albers would not have approved.

Book Review

Drapery, Classicism and Barbarism in Visual Culture
Gen Doy

Book Review

Drapery, Classicism and Barbarism in Visual Culture by Gen Doy (I.B. Taurus, 2002)

The significance of drapery and the draped body has until recently seemed a marginalized and neglected realm within critiques of visual culture. Despite its raised status from that of mere "cloth" through the traditions of visual art, and its transcendent passage through the depreciating effects of the demise of classical art in the early twentieth century, the "anatomy" of drapery has remained largely unexplored as a subject in its own right. Gen Doy, Professor of the History of Visual Culture at De Montfort University, Leicester has played a key role in addressing this neglect.

Drapery: Classicism and Barbarism in Visual Culture is timely and thought provoking. In conjunction with its release, and coinciding with Anne Hollander's *Fabric of Vision* exhibition at London's National Gallery, Doy organized an interdisciplinary conference, *Drapery in Visual Culture: Contexts, Clothing and Corporealities*. Doy further curated an exhibition of contemporary art at the City Gallery, Leicester: *Fold: Drapery in Contemporary Visual Culture,* with an accompanying catalog. *Drapery* is therefore one element within a network of cultural events.

The book examines changing representations and the role of drapery in architecture, sculpture, painting, dress, dance, and photography. Amongst the rich fabric of ideas and an exuberance of facts, numerous illustrations of the work of both historical and contemporary visual artists are embroidered into the folds of this informative, but regrettably monochrome, publication. Doy has effectively woven the warp threads of mainly European historical visual culture with the weft threads of contemporary visual culture, from the earlier influences of classicism, which posited drapery as a "signifier of civilisation," to more recent, more controversial associations with photojournalism, transforming drapery into a "signifier of barbarism."

Drapery and the fold are primarily familiar as a textile model of the kind implied by garments. In this role the forms and maneuvers of drapery and the fold, form

Textile, Volume 1, Issue 1, pp. 204–208
Reprints available directly from the Publishers.
Photocopying permitted by licence only.
© 2003 Berg. Printed in the United Kingdom.

VIEWED BY CHRISTINE ALLMAN

sculpted layers of manufactured second skins. Mediating between the body and its surroundings, drapery provides a universal language giving humans their anthropological, social, and religious identity, a sense of being. These associations and meanings encourage a gradually broadening role for drapery whereby its traditional status is transcended, particularly through reference to postmodern and late-twentieth-century theory. Doy references the exhibition and accompanying catalog *Starke Falten (Strong Folds)* held in 1995 in the Museum Bellerive, Zurich, in which artists, photographers, weavers, and writers concerned with nature, dress, architecture, and the psychology of folds and pleats reflect this shift in status.

In a key chapter Doy intuitively reviews the work of the French psychiatrist and photographer Gaëtan de Clerambault (1872–1934), acknowledging the seduction of his fascinating work (both text and photographic images) whilst inviting the reader to consider the "author" and "some of the material conditions in which the subjects of Clerambault's research encountered the doctor." These images confront the the subtle boundaries between the "civilization" and "barbarism" of her central argument.

Doy explores the work of Lia Cook, among others, provoking a reminder of the relationship between drapery, the history of cloth production, and the materiality of cloth. She expresses the temptation to emphasize drapery as "materialised" in a literal sense, which she suggests would resist the prevailing trends of some

contemporary theorists concerned with the intangible, the ambiguou and the "in-between." Perhaps Cook's work resides appropriately somewhere in between "the abstract" and the "concrete;" Doy resists her own reservations and recognizes the complexity of the role of drapery as remaining objectively and poignantly "in-between."

This objectivity remains in her appraisal of the relationship between drapery, postmodernism, and the baroque. She discusses a implied comparison between the baroque impulse of anti-rational and anti-enlightenment approache in culture and society in relation to twentieth-century postmodern attitudes. This in turn suggests a change in approach to our place within the social and material worl and to notions of history and subjectivity. Doy critically examine the work of writers that have explored these areas and underlines the importance of the post-structuralist philosopher Gille Deleuze and his book *The Fold: Liebniz and the Baroque.*

Deleuze would argue that the considerable qualities of the movement of draped and folded cloth excite a magical theater of forms and maneuvers, a folding phenomenon related to perception and to a reflective consciousness which is "of the soul." This sugges a new concept of folding, no longe as pictorial or representational apparatus, but as a way of thinking and understanding the world removed from the rigidity of reason and logic, the considered characteristics of Enlightenment science and art. However, despite Deleuze's persuasive and creative

proach to drapery and the fold
d the interesting comparisons
th the symptomatic
agmentations of our times, Doy's
ppreciation of his theories is not
together convincing, reinforcing
er suggestively disapproving
ance at the idealism she
sociates with some contemporary
inkers.

Finally, the reader encounters
apery in the "common," the
amiliar" and yet mutating and
ntroversial role as a signifier of
arbarism, particularly as identified
thin photojournalism. She
amines explicit images of victims
terror, torture, war, famine, and
overty, reflecting on the way in

which the common experience of
violence, suffering, and death wraps
and drapes human bodies in soiled
and bloodied cloth, enclosing and
exhuming the margins between skin
and cloth.

Doy offers the reader the
opportunity to question the
inclusion of these images within a
study of drapery, confronting the
boundaries and structures of what
is understood and accepted as
contemporary visual culture. To
conclude the work Doy quotes the
words of Walter Benjamin to
reinforce the resulting paradox:
(t)here is no document of civilisation
which is not at the same time a
document of barbarism.

Initially, *Drapery* reads as a vast
patchwork of interrelated material in
which an attempt to identify a
consistent pattern of inquiry can
result in frustration. However, after
closer scrutiny one is left with
admiration at the skill and ambition
of the author in facing the
identification and recording of the
complex configurations and
changing role of drapery within
visual culture. One can only
recommend this publication to
writers, makers and art historians
and suggest that any frustration
should provoke action to participate
in further making and further
exploration of the "anatomy of
drapery and the fold."